Famines and Face Packs

Famines and Face Packs

Emma Stratton

Copyright © 2003 Emma Stratton

First published in 2003 by Spring Harvest Publishing Division and
Authentic Lifestyle

09 08 07 06 05 04 03   7 6 5 4 3 2 1

Authentic Lifestyle is an imprint of Authentic Media
PO Box 300, Carlisle, Cumbria, CA3 0QS, UK
Box 1047, Waynesboro, GA 30830-2047
www.paternoster-publishing.com

British Library Cataloguing in Publication Data
A catalogue record for this book is available from the British Library

ISBN 1-85078-480-9

Cover design by Diane Bainbridge
Printed in Great Britain by
Cox and Wyman, Reading, Berkshire

This book is dedicated to

Nick and Kevin
12/11/99

Contents

Kates and Bex.
Katy, I know you wanted a book about horses,
and
Bex, you wanted Postman Pat and Jess to be in it –
sorry!
I hope you enjoy it anyway – at some point.

Love you girls. Lots.
Aunty Em XXX

Acknowledgements

Mummy and Daddy – Thank you for parenting me to have wings, thank you even more for encouraging, supporting and loving me enough to have the confidence to use them.

Sara – Few sisters surely feel as well loved when they are miles from home as they do at home. Thank you for loving me any time, any place. Love you too.

Ali – For your belief, patience, support, talent – and for taking a risk.

Tearfund – For being an organisation whose mission statement I am proud to refer to as ours.

For the opportunity to write, and that you actually said 'yes' – I'm still floored by that!

DRT – For the commitment, motivation and professionalism the team has shown me – some of it might even rub off on me one day.

For colleagues who I now call friends.

Rozzy – For offering me the time, space, sand, sea air and much needed hospitality. For your positive, honest, valued and sound feedback, delivered with lashings of grace and gentleness – how do you do that? For believing this book has been worth writing, and even worth reading!

Dave – For your support, friendship and unfaltering encouragement.

Sa – It was your comment after reading my first draftiest of draft chapters that swayed my decision to write. Thanks for that, bud. Thank you for your unconditional friendship – Albrecht Durer and Franz Knigstein would be proud! Ooh, and thanks for promising to buy a few copies – appreciate it, Sa!

Introduction

Writing this book, I did have a few moments of particularly limited optimism. Reassured, however, by timely support from many of my nearest and dearest that there was a point to my fumbling literary efforts, and that they would guarantee at least thirty-seven sales of the finished product, I carried on.

There was the relatively disconcerting email I had from Ali, my Commissioning Editor. She informed me that, at the ripe old age of twenty-eight, I could not punctuate 'its'! I was using the right letters – which was some comfort – but the whole apostrophe thing baffled me beyond belief – and that was only a three letter word! I also discovered that I habitually mis-spell 'privelidge', 'embaress', and I still don't know whether it's 'bear with me' or 'bare with me' – as in 'tarry with me'. And this is my mother tongue!!

I type with my middle fingers and thumbs. Occasionally, when I'm feeling particularly risqué, I splash out with a flamboyant gesture on 'o', 'p', or 'i' with my right little finger! Touch-typing without checking out the screen leads to cryptic results that code breakers would be unable to crack.

Perhaps these are not the soundest of emotional, cognitive and physical platforms on which to decide to write a book! However, the opportunity came along … I couldn't say 'no'. I thought about it, briefly. Too briefly to twig that a few emails home and scrawling a cathartic diary whilst working away had actually been a tad easier than the task of sitting down and tapping out around 60,000 entertaining and poignant words.

At the moments of more heady egotistical excursions, I've had to go back to the reasons I started writing this in the first place; to keep myself tied to what I wanted and still want the book to do, to show, to tell. I hope you'll find enough honesty in these pages to be assured that although some of the stories may be unusual, the settings – exceptional, the events – bizarre; that doesn't make me in any way unusual, exceptional and bizarre. From an early age my mum has assured me that I am 'special'. Though said with love, I've never been fully convinced that it is a compliment! My dream, my prayer, is that these pages will affect you. The times I've written about have affected me. They have challenged, entertained, hurt, angered and upset me, shown me hope, made me laugh, cry and despair. That's what I want this book in some way to do to you. It's a big ask but I'm asking it!

When this was in its embryonic stages, I wrote to Ali, desperately trying to articulate what I hoped it might be

> …I just do not want this book to become something it was never meant to be. I need and want to watch the pedestal placing that is easy to slip into when you work in 'exciting places, doing exciting things'. I want this book to be a story that opens eyes, and challenges hearts, that makes people think, cry, and laugh all at once; that lets people see the 'normal' face of a Christian girl, not the super-spiritual or the sacrificial – but the day-to-day stuff, struggles and joys. Nothing more and nothing less than that really. It's the 'here and now' of 'there and then' – Sudan, Kosovo and Serbia.

I started doing relief work because I wanted to 'change the world', and had the audacity to believe I could. Three and a half years later, I've realised it's not been that way round at all. Relief work has had a greater effect on me than I on it, on the way I think and behave, the way I view myself, other people, the 'world', God, everything. It has been an incredible few years. I've loved it; at times I've also hated it. It has answered questions, but has thrown up a load more, which are as yet unanswered. At times I have been angered and despairing of what I have seen or heard. I've also found hope and encouragement in some unexpected situations. Though I have been apart from my family and friends, I've been welcomed into many communities. On occasions I have been closer to God than ever before. I've also lost sight of him, only to find him again in the unlikeliest places.

It's my hope that this book offers glimpses not only of the dramatic, the 'drum' from 1999-2002; but also some of the ordinary, the 'hum' of those years, and how I have seen them.

I've been struck whilst writing that the way I have represented events might not be anything like the way anyone else would tell them. Memory seems an interesting phenomenon, and I'm aware that mine is not purely objective, but is a complex mixing pot involving my attitudes, thoughts and personality. Those facets shape what I remember, and therefore what I have written. I tell no story but my own, because it's the only one I know how to tell! These thoughts and spurious ramblings are not those of Tearfund. They are mine.

Some of the text is log or diary based, written at the time and sent home to friends and family. Alistair Cooke does his *Letters from America*; in this age of technological wizardry I did 'emails from Sudan'. These parts – in smaller print – are undoctored, complete with typos, grammatical creativity, previously undiscovered words (like undoctored), etc. The rest was written later. These are more reflective – well, that's the theory. Grammatical creativity? Quite possibly.

Enjoy.

Photo: Sarah Casey

Chapter 1

Looking for Relief

Renes and I had both graduated from Chester College the year before. Since then she had become a newly qualified member of the teaching profession. I'd pushed on to Exeter and was studying sport psychology. I had just finished the taught year of my course with my dissertation year looming ahead. In the meantime, we both had what we feared might be one of our last long summer holidays stretching ahead. The pressure was on: it had to be a good one.

'My aunt and uncle are Salvation Army officers, working in Bangladesh,' Renes ventured. 'I want to go out and visit – you up for it?'

'Yup.'

Not the most protracted dialogue in the world, but its outcome has markedly influenced my life. We went to Bangladesh.

★ ★ ★ ★

I'd become a Christian earlier that year. It was a reluctant buckling. My two closest friends at Chester (Renes and Heather) were both – to my dismay – Christians. I was in a blissful state of ignorant agnosticism, and not really that fussed either way! I set out to let them know that they were wasting their time with this 'irrelevant, untrue and implausible' faith of theirs.

I read about it. I enjoyed the culinary treats and cerebral challenges of an Alpha course, and heartily voiced my objections, my waterproof points on creation, evolution, etc that unfortunately leaked under scrutiny. I pooh-poohed sermons at their churches, sat silently through worship. I argued with them. I walked away from 'the God thing'.

But it didn't disappear. To my dismay, and indeed fear, pennies were beginning to drop. Issues were beginning to make an uncomfortable amount of sense when looked at through Christian glasses.

Undoubtedly the Ten Commandments seemed a sound framework to live by. There did seem to be weighty proof (from secular sources) that Jesus did walk the earth, that his teaching and ministry did turn people upside-down. The likelihood of a cosmic 'Big Bang' resulting in the dynamic and delicate bio-geo-chemical status of our earth being just so began to take more faith to believe than acknowledging that there might have been a Creator at work. Our earth being fallen, imperfect – BBC1 6pm daily gave evidence galore. Me being a sinner? – Yup. Not the worst of the bunch – surely! – but certainly, far from angelic.

The outcome of my unsuccessful quest to disprove the existence of God was on 23rd February 1997. Driving down the M5 from Crewe, I finally conceded. I'd got to a point where I had experienced too much of God to deny his existence any longer. It was taking more faith to deny him than to accept him! Having admitted that, I knew I needed to do something about it.

I got back to Exeter that night, and knocked on Jenny's door. Jenny lived in the room next to mine in our hall. I didn't know Jenny's surname, I still don't – I think I'd probably had four conversations with her up until then. I'd guessed she might be a Christian because every Sunday I'd be woken by her door closing at about 9-9:30. She was quite quiet and nice as well. Overwhelming evidence!

So, I put my bags in my room, and knocked on Jenny's door.

'Jenny, hi. I want to be a Christian, um ... what do I need to do?'

She looked shocked. I guess it's not every day that a relative stranger walks into your room and drops that on you. She seemed to get quite excited, started speaking very quickly, but didn't actually say very much at all. I began to wonder whether this was a good idea. As I toyed with the idea of forgetting the whole thing, she suggested we pray. We did. That was that. I can't remember the details of the prayer – something along the lines of:

Sorry – for the things Em has done wrong in her life. Thank you – that you died on the cross for her, to forgive her. Please – by your Spirit come into her life. My sole verbal contribution was 'Amen'. In a terribly British way I thanked her and left! Jenny moved out of the hall a few weeks later. I haven't seen her since.

Sara, my sister, called later. I was wondering what on earth I'd just done, fretting over how much I'd need to change my lifestyle, how I was going to tell people, and chuckling inanely occasionally in pure relief that the weight of what I can only describe as feeling like a fight that I'd been involved in had ceased. Sara was badgering me for an answer about whether I'd be Kate's (my niece) godmother. She'd been asking for weeks, and I'd fobbed her off, feeling that for me to stand up in church and say that I would:

- Pray regularly for her
- Set her an example of Christian living
- Help her to grow in the faith of God, Father, Son and Holy Spirit, in which she was baptised
- Give every encouragement to her to follow Christ and to fight against evil
- Help her to look forward to her confirmation

... would make a mockery of what Renes and Heather believed. But I SO wanted to do it. I'd managed for weeks not to say 'no' to Sara, nor to say 'yes'. This Sunday evening my time was up. Plans needed to be finalised for the christening, she had to have an answer one way or the other. I could now make and mean those statements. I said 'yes'.

When Renes asked a few months later about heading off to Bangladesh for a chance to see this global church that I had just committed myself to 'in action', it was with wide-eyed enthusiasm that I boarded the plane. I knew we'd get involved in work out there, but I did not know my eyes would be so dramatically peeled open by what I saw, nor that my ignorant perceptions of the 'Third World' would be so vigorously rattled. I did not anticipate that when I reboarded the plane from Dhaka to the UK a few weeks later, with a large wicker chair, four foot stools, two hammocks, and Renes' rather splendid full size papier mâché goose, that it would be the non-material mementoes that would be the starkest memories of our trip.

First impression from the air:

The land has sunk. It's submerged. Everywhere you look is river, land under water, or land perilously close to being under water.

Second impression, the road to Dhaka:

You cannot swing a cat here, not even a hamster. It is packed, absolutely heaving, every hour is rush hour.

Third impression, in Dhaka:

I saw a beggar beside the road and began a silent conversation with myself whilst I sat in traffic, trying not to look but unable to draw my eyes away from him. He's got no legs and no arms. Why's that then? How do you lose all your limbs? Polio? A traffic accident? Rickets? Leprosy?

A small boy was with him, maybe seven years old, nipping through the traffic with a plastic tub. Rapping on car windows, he'd point to the man who was propped up against a wall. At times the smooth mechanisation of tinted windows would be activated, and a hand would drop small change into his tub. Other times, horns would be sounded, a scornful hand would wave him on, people would deliberately avoid eye contact – as I did. One driver even felt the need to swipe him firmly round the head.

I saw the man and boy several times. I saw the man roll in the dirt to move around. I saw the boy giving him a drink, holding the cup to his mouth and the dilapidated skateboard platform that the boy would lift or drag the man onto when they needed to move further than his shuffling efforts could shift him.

Sometimes I dropped small change. But at other times I found the view 180 degrees from the man and boy more absorbing, and offered them the back of my head. Sometimes my tears flowed, and my anger boiled at the lack of support and justice, the degrading conditions that they lived in. But at other times I was untouched – I could just walk on by.

We visited several brothels where the Sally Army had initiated health care and alternative income generation projects. Communities of women and children, in the business of sex; not the pleasure of sex that our western culture advocates, but just business. Children – born of their mother's clients – would lie drugged (ensuring they slept

soundly) under beds whilst their mothers worked above them. Girls of
ten would be welcomed into apprenticeship in the family business.
Career choices? Possibilities to opt out? Not a reality. Not for an illiter-
ate, 'spoiled' girl. Time, money and hope would not be wasted on
non-vocational education. Training would be 'on the job'.

One of the lady's rooms we visited had a poster in it – a cute fluffy
kitten with a pastel yellow ribbon around its neck. There weren't cute
fluffy kittens in the brothel. If the picture surprised me, the text at the
bottom of it blew us away.

The Lord Will Provide (Gen. 22:14)

Does he?

Was he?

Here?

How?

Born into a brothel, fatherless, STDs[1] high on the probability list,
trapped – the Lord providing? Not my idea of provision!

A few months before, I'd got to that point of having enough answers
to commit to Christianity. In Bangladesh questions, albeit new questions, seemed to be on the rise. Answers were few and unsatisfactory. I
remember standing on the flat roof of the house we were staying in. Two
storms were brewing, a meteorological brute and an emotional tempest.
Thunder crashed, lightning lit up the sky, and rain drove into my face.
Standing there drenched, I yelled at God in absolute frustration at the
state of some of the lives we'd seen, at the fact that I was about to get
on a plane and just walk on by, at the lack of justice and equity, and at
my uselessness in it all. Absolutely marvellous – there I was about to
return to my studies of how to get more people more active more often,
and improve somebody's tennis performance by working on their mental game, whilst being racked by what I'd seen in Bangladesh.

I came back keen to do something about what I had seen. Having
witnessed the poverty and oppression of so many Bangladeshi people, I
could not settle back into Exeter. I don't believe that a career in sport
or exercise is wrong. Had the Olympic selectors had my telephone

---

[1] Sexually transmitted diseases

number, I'd have willingly served my country in a lycra suit! But it felt absolutely wrong for me to bury my head in journals, and leave Bangladesh behind. Studying was the last thing in the world I wanted to do, which made it tricky – it was the only thing in the world I was supposed to be doing that September! I must have been a nightmare to live with, wanting to change the world. I was so far from the here and now, totally absorbed in the there and then.

My dissertation, on how much physical activity children did during their break-times, did not really progress at all that first term. I wrote to aid agencies galore offering my services as a volunteer. The replies that did come back had a remarkably common thread!

Dear Emma

Many thanks for your letter …
Unfortunately we don't have any opportunities for people with no experience …
Should you gain any experience we'd be delighted to hear from you again …
Wishing you every success …
Yours faithfully,
Relief organisation, inundated with numerous similar optimistic yet unrealistic requests!

It wasn't the most promising of starts to a career change. One of my church leaders suggested trying Tearfund's Disaster Response Team. My experience of Tearfund dated back about fifteen years to a campaign of theirs that my Sunday school supported.

I wrote in April – they sent an application form. I filled it in – they invited me for an initial interview – result! I was initially interviewed – they invited me back for the real interview in July. With four other people, we constructed a newspaper tower without talking to each other, watched videos of Tearfund's work and had a delicious lunch. My professional suitability, personal and spiritual maturity were explored. In spite of that, I was accepted on the Register. It must have been the newspaper tower that swung it. The Register is not a job offer, it's a database of people who may be asked to go on an assignment. I kept a bag of essentials packed expectantly.

Five expectant months later, February 1999, I got a call from personnel. Would I go to southern Sudan for a three month assignment as a seeds and tool logistician?

'Yes, of course – fantastic!'

The Personnel Officer suggested I take a little time to think and pray about it and chat it through with family and friends. I agreed but I knew I'd go! I knew nothing about Sudan, had no logistical experience other than organising children's summer play schemes, and as for the seeds and tool element? – my Girl Guide flower arranging badge was the peak of my horticultural efforts. In spite of that, it just did not cross my mind to say no.

I said 'yes'.

Seed and tool distribution in Sudan
Photo: Emma Stratton

Chapter 2

Into Africa ...

Having been briefed up to the eyeballs and prayed out of the door by the UK based team at the Tearfund offices in Teddington, it was with much poorly concealed excitement that I rattled through my goodbyes. In all of the build-up to leaving the UK, I didn't get bothered by the responsibility of co-ordinating the distribution of seeds and tools to ten thousand families in one of the most remote, geographically inhospitable, war-torn regions of the world. Even the sobering practicality of writing a will did little to quash my zeal. It was all too big an adventure to get spooked by. It was as though in my naïve enthusiasm, another gear of living had been found. This was what I had impatiently waited for, the chance to get out there and get on with 'it'.

I took off from Heathrow on 8th February 1999. With the prospect of eight hours or so on board, I made the most of the on-board services provided. I sprawled out on four unused seats, cocooned myself in all four blankets, headphones on, donned an eye-mask, and was particularly delighted by the royal blue and cerise towelling sockettes that may still, to this day, be hot-footing around southern Sudan.

Another Tearfund 'rookie' (Phil) and I hotelled a short distance from the Nairobi office for the first few nights. A whole room to myself – surely the height of international travel! We went down to the restaurant for dinner, and were somewhat perturbed by the fact that when we returned, both our rooms had been broken into and our stuff rifled through. Perhaps broken into is the wrong phrase – there was no sign of a forced entry. An inside job? Phil had had some money stolen, but that was it. Though relieved, I did feel strangely offended that the criminal did not deem any of my possessions worth nicking. The money was not recovered, but a man walking around the hotel grounds later that night was severely beaten by the police in spite of the total lack of evidence linking him to the crime.

Tearfund's southern Sudan programme

Following its inception in 1998, this was increasing in size at the start of 1999. Along with half a dozen other new team members recruited from Nairobi, our first few days were based in the city for orientation and induction. My desire to get into Sudan had become a growing itch, but towards the end of the orientation came the bad news that the security situation in Mike Kilo was poor, and therefore it would not be possible to fly in for a few days.

However, we were able to drive a brand spanking new vehicle up the backbone of Kenya through the Rift Valley to Lokichokio where it was to be flown out to our project site, a two-day trip. Rob and I shared the drive. He was my project co-ordinator, my boss. By the time we got to Loki we were getting on well enough for him not to fulfil his threat of putting me 'on the next flight out'. The drive was phenomenal, spectacular scenery, minimal traffic, beautiful weather.

The majority of relief programmes in southern Sudan are operated out of Nairobi. Strategy co-ordination meetings are held there; the UN, programme-funding donors and other NGOs (non-governmental organisations – like Tearfund) are all represented there. Lokichokio, a Turkana town on the Kenyan-Sudanese border is next, the logistics base; a three-hour flight or two-day drive from Nairobi. In 1999 almost everyone and everything relief-related entering or leaving southern Sudan from Kenya went through Loki, transient home to the assortment of 'Mercenaries, Misfits, Madmen and Missionaries' that choose to stay, for their honourable and less honourable motives, in disaster-riddled, war-torn places.

Loki was the entrance and exit point for relief workers going into Sudan (the field). After six or so weeks of work, rest and recuperation was taken (R&R). Relief workers were flown down to Nairobi to relax in Kenya. It's not easy in Nairobi; but the coast, the lakes, safari parks –

it's quite hard not to relax in a country of such beauty. Then back up to Loki, and the cycle began again. Loki was the last place to access tapped water, air-conditioning, cold beer or cold anything, chairs with cushions on or telephones. Part hub of a well-established, multimillion dollar relief operation, part MASH-style camp, part prison with its perimeter fencing and security, part den of iniquity – Loki was a place of many faces.

Like many of the Loki offices, Tearfund's was a large converted container, with one window, two doors, a large identifying Tearfund sticker and a hammock outside for the daily siestas. Furnishings totalled a couple of desks, four chairs, a big book case, a laptop, paper trays and files galore, wall maps riddled with allegedly strategically based pins, a satellite telephone, numerous GP300 handsets for short distance radio communications, and a high-frequency (HF) radio set for talking with Nairobi and the different project sites in Sudan.

Sudan is a country at war with itself. Since 1955 there has only been peace for one decade. It boasts, with little pride, a speculated greater number of human casualties than the combined death toll of the Rwandan and Chechnyan conflicts. Since 1983, two million people have died because of the war, and four million have had to move from their homes. A massive 92 per cent of the population live below the internationally recognised poverty line.

The war rolls on, the south wanting independence from the north. The stakes have been massively exacerbated in recent years with the discovery of rich oil fields. The north versus south picture, though, is too simplistic. Within the south are many tribal groups, with a bloody history of inter-tribal fighting for power, control and land rights.

The relief effort operates in an active war zone. Safety and security of relief workers are high on the agenda. Plans and procedures for 'what to do if ...' are written up, drilled into people, updated, implemented and revised. For the majority of NGOs, the UN has responsibility to inform and arrange the evacuation of personnel when judged appropriate. It all sounds exhilarating, but the disruption to local relationships and project work is massive, not to mention the stress of living with the constant threats of danger.

Sudan is a country at war with itself
Photo: Richard Hanson, Tearfund

In February, the dry season, Sudan was brown. A GAP khaki brown,
with occasional bursts of green tree canopies, randomly scattered. River
beds meandered casually along their lazy courses, so casually they were
dry; river beds without the river. And it was flat, contourless, a doddle
for an Ordnance Survey cartographer! The flight from Loki into
Malualkon, our destination, took three hours. Known affectionately to
all as Mike Kilo, it is in the county of Aweil East, home to the Dinka
tribe, tall, lean, dignified pastoralists.

As the plane approached the air strip, it circled the Dinka village;
mud huts with grass roofs, a water pump crowded with women in
bright coloured wraps, a few large fenced-off compounds of a number
of huts. Rob pointed out the landmarks; the Tearfund compound of

tents, mud huts and its long distinctive stores, a few narrow tracks criss-crossing, and a long straight dirt road built by the Brits in the 1950s, stretching from east to west.

The plane was met by a large crowd. One guy had a wheelbarrow and our bags were trundled off to the compound. There was so much, too much to try and take in – how black the people were, how many smiling faces, the heat, the naked children touching your arm whilst you walked to see if the 'white' would rub off, the heat, the welcoming speechettes of various local dignitaries, the heat, the stares, the unfamiliar language, the heat, not knowing where anything was or how to get anywhere. I grinned inanely, shook hands repeatedly, stuck close to Rob and the others from the plane, and grinned some more.

Tearfund Mike Kilo

We walked the five minutes through the village to the compound, into something of an oasis of tranquillity. Inside only the Tearfund team, staff and invited guests had access – our place. It was divided into three sections:

- Outer – the stores, where kit and equipment and oil, sugar, unimix (the high energy, nutritious soya based mix that we distributed in the feeding programme) etc were stored – the items necessary for the project to operate.
- Middle – the office, team food store, vehicle parking and team eating area. Only team members and local staff involved directly with these areas were allowed in this section.
- Inner – the teams' sleeping quarters, loo and shower block. The team only area.

The immediate striking feature was the tree. It must have been the biggest in Mike Kilo. One of the churches used to meet under it but offered Tearfund its shade and the immediate surrounding area on which to build the compound. It served as a landmark in my early days. It could be seen from much of the village and many were the times I appreciated its shade. February was the height of the dry season; we reached 52 degrees Celsius one day! In that kind of temperature your body just clamours to stop. The Sudan sun at its hottest is a real enemy. I have a sun-loving reputation developed through summers running around naked on the beach (predominantly during my infant years!), but I quickly started slapping on the cream, covering up with loose cottons and planning my routes around the village with maximal tree cover and minimal mileage.

Our mud-walled, thatched-roofed homes were called tuckles. I was in a tent, though, whilst I was there. The interior furnishings were a goat-skin strung bed and accompanying mozzy net, some shelves for clothes, a small table and – depending on your status within the team – a chair or a foot stool. My foot stool was small. Such simple living, a rucksack worth of personal kit, was great.

The Tearfund team consisted of a Ugandan nutritionist, an Ethiopian community health educator, two Kenyan nurses, a Brit compound manager, a Sudanese food security officer, a Brit project co-ordinator, and me with the auspicious title of 'seeds and tools logistician'. There were also over twenty Sudanese staff, feeding assistants, water carriers, educators, compound workers, drivers, cooks and cleaners. Some spoke English, others did not and my Dinka linguistic skills were poor. However, we can communicate and understand one another a lot more than I'd realised without words. Some of my favourite 'conversations' involved mime skills that have enhanced my Christmas charade ability massively.

- Two arms outstretched from the shoulders accompanied by a mechanical humming noise – an aeroplane
- One arm held out in front of me, the other arm jumping over the top of it – tomorrow
- Either arm held at a considered angle in the sky – indicative of the position of the sun – time of day
- Pretending to receive a package from someone – the mail pouch from the pilot
- Put it all together – a request to pick up the mail pouch from the incoming flight ETA 'whatever' time tomorrow.

Admittedly there is room for error in all that, and it was relatively time
consuming – but it was good fun.

★ ★ ★ ★

The project had been set up in October 1998 in response to the high
rates of malnutrition in the area and had a three-pronged approach to
its work. The medical vulnerability of the elderly and the young to disease and malnourishment is intensified within the Sudanese culture. It
is the man of the house who gets first shout on food, therefore younger
children are particularly vulnerable to the effects of food deficits. The
immediate feeding needs of under-fives were met by weekly targeted
distributions from supplementary feeding centres in six different locations throughout the county. Poor health practices augmented the
effects of food shortages; for example, drinking unclean water could
induce diarrhoea. Teams of local health educators would encourage
communities to adopt less risky behaviours, such as filtering water or
not using stagnant ponds.

Food security aims to provide a more medium term solution to
situations of food shortages, to 'feed for life by teaching fishing, rather
than feeding for a day by giving fish.' In the project this included the
distribution of fishing kits, education in crop growing, and the seeds and
tool distribution, which is where my work fitted in. The time pressure
was to get the distributions completed in time for the planting season,
to allow sowing to occur at about the time of the first rains. Too soon,
and the seeds might be eaten by recipients to meet their immediate
hunger needs; too late, and it might not be possible for the planes
freighting in the seeds and tools to land because of a boggy airstrip. It
was tricky to predict the exact dates with any accuracy. The cows in
Mike Kilo were lying down and standing up sporadically with
seemingly no regard to the fact that they were one of my primary
meteorological forecasting tools.

Another issue affecting timing was security. The last thing we
wanted was the compound sitting full of seeds and tools if there was the
possibility we'd have to evacuate before completing the distribution.
They were valuable commodities, especially in the quantity that we had
on board. The middle section of the compound was at one stage well

carpeted with two hundred rows' worth of fifty sacks of packages. Relationships with the community were really good, but having that quantity of items, both in terms of economic and immense practical value, sitting inside our grass fence perimeter could have put an awful lot of temptation into the equation.

★ ★ ★ ★

The insecurity that had postponed our arrival in Mike Kilo had passed. Warawar, a village to our north, bore the scars. Part had been torched during an attack – torching a mud hut with a dried grass roof leaves a predictable outcome. The first afternoon we arrived, Rob wanted to talk with the local leaders and see if any assistance was necessary. I was overwhelmed by the heat, the apparent lack of road and trepidation over what we'd see at the village.

Alison was next to me – Tearfund's community health education co-ordinator. She'd been with the programme for six months and I was floored by how relaxed she seemed. As though six squashed people bouncing along in a 4x4 listening to a language you didn't understand in sweltering heat in the middle of nowhere heading towards a village that had been burning a few days ago was the most normal thing in the world. Als was in Mike Kilo for all of my first week before heading off elsewhere. She was a real support, managing to strike a balance of introducing, telling and showing, and letting me learn by myself.

Driving into Warawar, it was immediately evident which part of the village had suffered. The mud huts were now just charred walls. They were close together so the fire must have easily danced from one hut to the next. Although the fire was just days ago, people were already rebuilding. Some just needed to re-roof, while other huts were so damaged that total reconstruction was necessary. I was struck by the reaction of many. Rather than anger or mournful resignation, there seemed to be an incredible sense of pragmatic acceptance. In Sudan, it happens, in what is already a climatically inhospitable land where a war has raged for years. There's a big difference between resignation – being beaten by it, and acceptance – acknowledging that that is how it is, but getting on with it as best you can. A whole generation has grown up knowing only war in southern Sudan and have seen little sign of imminent peace, yet life goes on.

Ethiopia '85 provided the first pictures of hungry people I remember seeing. I enthusiastically joined Bob Geldof's *Run the World*, lolloping along the Jersey coastline with the crowds. I watched the six o'clock news by myself one night with tears coursing down my cheeks. My reaction in Sudan, though, was starkly different. I remember feeling incredibly concerned and guilty over my lack of emotion. Hard-hearted? Maybe. A coping strategy? Probably.

As part of my orientation to the project, in my first week I visited a couple of the supplementary feeding centre sites. Saturday was Mike Kilo's day. The children brought to the centre were weighed and measured, and given a medical check on their health from the project nurses. Questions were asked about food availability, eating habits and diarrhoea, with a view to minimising further bouts of illness and exploring possibilities of accessing other food sources. If the child was ill, they would be referred to the local primary health care clinic run by another Mike Kilo based NGO. If, for a number of weeks, the child had consistently maintained their weight at the target level for their height, they would be discharged from the feeding programme, or, if according to weight for height standards – or other nutritional indicators – they were assessed as being malnourished, they would be admitted to the feeding programme, given an identity bracelet and number and issued with a week's worth portion of unimix to be made into porridge. They would have some time with the nurses encouraging positive nutritional practices, and be asked to revisit next week.

One of the ways I coped with the daily scenes of suffering around us was to rationalise situations; a kind of logical detachment from sentimentality. There aren't many vents for it in that kind of environment. At home, after a bad day at work, I'd have walked the beach, called a friend, belted a squash ball round a court. In Sudan, if you walk, you're accompanied by children. Your friends are your team mates, coping with similar stuff in their own ways. The best you could do was jog with that same posse of giggling children at your heels daring one another to try and touch you.

I had to develop a new repertoire of coping skills – one was this rationalisation of situations; another, a commitment to work at what was within my sphere of control – to get on with my bit, and accept that which I couldn't change. I learnt to write as well. Originally I thought I was doing it to keep people at home in touch. But I found that putting on paper the events, and to a lesser extent my attached thoughts and to a still lesser extent, my feelings, acted as a real cathartic release for me. I love being heard in my friendships. Conversation is great, but with some things, I don't need or want people to respond. I simply want to be heard, and in the absence of verbal communication, writing was my only way of knowing that I would be.

★ ★ ★ ★

'Echo Sierra what is your position, over?'

'Just leaving Whisky Romeo heading for Mike Kilo, ETA twenty-five minutes.'

'Hold your position until further notice, copy that?'

'Copy.'

I still remember the conversation, detecting the edge of urgency and concern in Rob's voice; still remember the tangible surge of adrenaline and involuntary acceleration of my heart rate. In spite of being with a driver, a local counterpart security man and the vehicle being surrounded by a crowd, I felt utterly and absolutely alone.

It was probably only about fifteen minutes, but my brain went into overdrive. Insecurity. I had heard about it, done some training, been held up at 'gun point' by enthusiastic balaclavaed volunteers during training, heard the tales of various incidents that had become folklore. There seemed to me to be an air of stripe earning about the whole thing. Until now, I had had an almost romantic image of fleeing from a pursuing enemy, and naturally, in my mind, the stories always ended up happily ever after.

The security threats in Sudan at the time were mainly ground based. Mike Kilo was in rebel-held territory 'governed' by the SPLA, the Sudanese Peoples Liberation Army, I always felt rebel was a bit strong, but it was non-government aligned. The government of Sudan (GoS) therefore would at times launch major ground-based offensives to claim back various towns in the south. A train would pass along the track forty kilometres to the west of Mike Kilo, from north to south, throughout the dry season carrying weapons, supplies and soldiers to bolster the handful of government-held towns and garrisons in the south. The train was accompanied by government soldiers but also by the PDF (People's Defence Force), often on horseback. Naturally, the train was a target for the SPLA. On its return journey north, the empty train would allegedly carry plunder from villages that troops had attacked. These villages tended to be within a relatively narrow corridor near to the railway that Mike Kilo was generally beyond. Invariably therefore, fighting and tension were constant when the train was on the move.

Tension had been high in Mike Kilo for the last few days. Longer serving team members were aware that the community seemed nervous. Rumours of potential invasion were rife and although of little substance, were never quite substance-less enough to ignore. Many villagers had packed their few possessions and the staff frequently nipped out of the compound to check on family members and stay abreast with news. Security procedures were tightened up, radio checks with Loki became more frequent, regular information-sharing meeting with other NGOs started, our 'quick run' back packs of various useful items and supplies necessary for sustaining life in the event of an emergency evacuation rarely left our sides. Mine was more substantial than most – alongside my compass, map, water bottle, purification tablets, first aid kit, food and spare radio battery went a few of what I felt to be 'essential luxury' items – chewing gum, deodorant, my photo album and a good book. I was thinking quality of life, as opposed to just life!

It was during my second week in Sudan, and I was on my way back from a village to the north when the instruction to hold my position came. Tearfund have a security plan in each location detailing potential risks, preventative measures, safety procedures and evacuation plans. I'd read it twice, but during those minutes holding my position in Warawar, knowing something was awry in Mike Kilo, yet clueless to the details, I made a mental note to re-reread the information asap. I mentally ran through the location of the 'quick run points' (places identified 1-2km from our compound to quickly run to if necessary). I stared at the radio microphone, finger poised on the button, wondering what was going on at base. Why hadn't Rob called back? Had they had to evacuate? Had anyone picked up any of my stuff? Eventually an incoming call rang through.

'Proceed to base directly.'

Having found our driver in the market, who had nipped off to get a couple of mangos (they were on special apparently), we proceeded very directly, managing to knock about a quarter off the usual journey time.

By the time we arrived back in Mike Kilo, the fever pitch had dropped. Rob relayed to me over a stiff mug of tepid water how the staff had fled the compound whilst telling members of the expat team to do likewise – the village was under attack. Villagers were running into the bush, bundles on heads, children scooped up, homes abandoned. The team prepared for an immediate overland evacuation, which is when Rob first called me on the radio.

It transpired that the trigger to this was a pack of wild dogs, rather than marauding assailants on horseback. The dogs ran through the village, pursued vigorously by a group of stone-throwing boys. Villagers saw the boys running and immediately assumed the enemy were at hand. They ran. Our staff understandably did likewise, and so on. That is the ongoing stress that the southern Sudanese of that area (and others) are living under.

It had been my first taste of the fear of insecurity – and the excitement; the fear of being in a situation over which I had so little control. I could follow the security plan and get to the right place to meet the team, but I think it was this incident that brought home to me the fact that I was indeed a stranger in a strange land at war, where I didn't really understand the rules of daily living.

* * * *

Rob's contract and time in Mike Kilo finished in March. I am amazed at the phenomenal rate that friendships and trust develop when you work, rest and play 'team'. In just that month, I'd grown not only to respect Rob as my manager, but really to enjoy the times we spent together as friends. I wasn't looking forward to him going, and I therefore wasn't looking forward to his replacement arriving – but she did.

Rob had a week to hand over to George, and during that time you could see him winding down. The day Rob left, the whole team bundled down to the airstrip in the back of the pick-up to wait for his plane. It was late, and a really hot day. I took myself off quietly and sat on a tree, and thought, prayed and watched. It was ridiculous, I'd only known this guy for one month and yet was finding the prospect of watching him leave harder than some of the goodbyes I'd done in the UK. I think trust was a big part of it. On a few occasions of insecurity I'd really had to trust Rob – his judgement, his leadership, his decision-making. With him leaving, I had to redevelop that trust from scratch in George.

The plane eventually circled lazily before trundling down the airstrip towards us. Goodbyes were said in the noisy dust and heat as the propellers whirred, and he was gone. I got back to the compound, George asked me a question about something or other, and I just burst in tears, quite an uncharacteristic response. The average length of contract with DRT is six to eight months. You get to say goodbye to a lot of colleagues and friends. You also get to meet a lot of new colleagues and potential friends.

The pain of saying goodbye to Rob was eased markedly by the speed that George and I became buddies. Once again, it was friendship at an accelerated rate. One of the best things about my time with Tearfund has been the friends I have been fortunate enough to make along the way. A very special bond of shared experience links people and, in many cases, holds a long way down the line.

Chapter 3

... Out of Africa

The totally alien quickly became my normality. I slotted into the swing of our daily routines. Up and shower, morning prayers and worship, breakfast together, brief chat about everyone's planned day, then off to work. Work for me varied from trips swapping locally grown seeds for food, receiving deliveries of hoes, sickles and sorghum seeds, packing and sorting, chatting with local authorities, refinding my often lost notebook, genning up on agricultural techniques, and so it went on. Lunch was often on the hoof. We stopped work between five and six, showered, I'd put on my PJs, we'd eat dinner as a team, and either chatted watching the stars, actively avoided playing Scrabble, read or wrote emails. I contemplated having a bash at the still unopened embroidery kit my mum had optimistically bought me, listened to music, played a bit of Jenga ... We weren't allowed out of the compound whilst it was dark for security reasons, and so could suffer from cabin fever. My life, however, was virtually all outside – so fresh air certainly wasn't lacking. We ate in the open air, I spent most of my working day outside and showered without a roof. I loved that side of things.

We worked a five and a half, sometimes six day week. Rarely, it became seven. If a flight was scheduled to arrive with seeds, tools or other supplies on a Sunday, naturally it needed unloading on a Sunday. Always there was the intention of taking a substitute day off as soon as possible. I was never very good at that bit though, as every other day of the week everyone else was working, so resting was not easy.

This is one area where my thinking has changed massively. Often the task then seemed so immense that a day off was unthinkable. Nowadays, the concept of a seven day week is foreign to me. We need the rest. I know now that in my eagerness to get it done, at some point reserves will run too low on all levels. I don't always get it right still, but am certainly a big ambassador of the six (and increasingly the five) day week. It is hard, though, in that kind of environment when you live where you work and the need is blatant. My work was never quite done, and it wouldn't be until ten thousand packages had been distributed.

* * * *

All the water we used was hand-pumped by two ladies employed just to collect water for the team. I felt quite uncomfortable with being served in this way, initially, so I enthusiastically strolled down to the pump with them one day to get my own. It's hard work. It took me at least twice as long as anyone else to fill my barrel. The two ladies were embarrassed by my indignant, awkward – and to their eyes insulting – efforts to pump. It was their livelihood, what gave them a level of status in the community, made them part of the Tearfund team. Selfishly and unrealistically, I had with the best of intentions tried to take that away from them. Unrealistic – because me going down to the pump, waiting for my turn, struggling to carry the barrels back to the compound, day in day out, would have left next to no time to do my job.

* * * *

Showering involved some resourcefulness. A vertically fixed corrugated metal sheet and concrete floored cubicle provided the necessary privacy. As a rule I used one half to two-thirds of a galvanised zinc bucket twice daily to wash. One of my physical treats of the day was pouring any excess in the bucket over my head, and really feeling spoilt! Fine unless you didn't hold the handle to the bucket and got a sharp clout as it swung into your forehead.

The shower had no roof, and the sky above Mike Kilo was unfathomably large. Most evenings the cosmos would put on a spectacular celestial display. I often used to find myself lost in the wonder of the stars. Mike Kilo geographically was not stunning, no lofty peaks, no sparkling lakes, no crashing waves, no inspiring flora and fauna. But the skies were where I could recognise God's hand, a great and much appreciated effort of the Lord on Day Four during that first creative week. Sunrise that would slowly pour out its light, sunset that would gently lower the place into darkness, the moon – the lesser light – that would govern the night, and the constant stars that would speckle the sky like an uncompleted dot to dot.

★ ★ ★ ★

Food was generally flown in from Loki. A month's worth of supplies at a time, all purchased in Kenya, were boxed up and sent along the logistical line into Mike Kilo. From time to time, a cool-box of fresh fruit and veg would arrive and be opened like a treasure trove: bananas, cabbage, maybe a pineapple, a few mangos, cabbage, potatoes, perhaps a water melon, cabbage. Within a day or two these scurvy-preventing consumables would have been duly consumed. There was next to nothing available to purchase locally with the exception of occasional mangoes, goats and chickens. Our diet was basic, and great efforts would be made by the team to jazz it up as much as possible.

Fruit trees were planted in the compound and efforts made to grow our own vegetables. Sweet potatoes did well, aubergine – a fine harvest, peppers – an abysmal disappointment. Our only other attempt at nutritional self-sufficiency was the chickens. Numbers of hens varied according to the team's appetite. Numbers of cocks varied according to team members' sleeping patterns. The chickens showed a total disregard to the outer, middle and inner section boundaries within the compound. They appeared to believe that they did rule the roost. The team were flexible with this to the point that any cock excessively 'doodle-dooing' in the hours considered too early was earmarked for the pot. It wasn't a rare sight to stumble out of my tent to find a red-eyed, bedraggled yet appeased-looking colleague heading for the kitchen with the offending bird swinging upside-down by the legs.

We'd often be called to the compound gate to check out the local livestock. I hadn't had much experience of assessing the quality of meat from a live animal before Sudan. They were inevitably a bit scrawny, yellow-toothed and their coats were neither shiny, nor were their noses damp and glistening with life – I learnt that from Peter Purves during his Crufts days with Petra. Goat could be boiled, fried, baked, roasted, stewed, anything at all really. The skin was saved, intestines (known affectionately as 'inner tubes'), various organs, tongue, were lovingly prepared. A goat could feed the team for about three days. The halitosis suffered from eating the goat would last for a further four. However the meat was cooked, it was never tender, and during a goat-eating week team jaw profiles would become radically enhanced as masticating muscles would develop because of intensive use. Thankfully, goat was a rare treat.

★ ★ ★ ★

There were no telecommunications in Mike Kilo. Our only communication links with life outside of Mike Kilo were the mail pouch and the radio. On a good day we could speak with Nairobi. Loki was generally clear and other Tearfund bases in southern Sudan were just a 'selcall' away. High frequency radio isn't private, therefore the radio was for functional messages only, information relaying of a non-sensitive nature, security checks and details of flight comings and goings. Friday nights, though, were of a different nature.

Phil was based in Billing, south of MK, as was Roz, the project coordinator. For about half an hour, our weekly banter through the airwaves was a real treat. It just normal inane chat, as normal as chat can be with 'over', 'copy that', and other airwave protocol necessities dropped in. I used to love it. It was a bonus to have some external contact. To be able to sit in one of the wobbly, green canvas director chairs in the office, throw back my head and laugh at various exploits was another of those simple treasured pleasures.

The mail pouch was a thick battered canvas bag with TEARFUND MIKE KILO embroidered onto it. Planes would come to Mike Kilo to drop off or pick up supplies or personnel as and when needed. Sometimes we could go for ten days without a flight. During the height of seeds and tools arriving, we had three planes in one day. Usually they came twice a week. Any plane flying overhead was worthy of attention, and I became something of a plane spotter:

Caravan = people coming/going
Buffalo   = people and/or supplies coming or going
Hercules = airdrop of unimix, cereal, sugar
Antonov = bombs (thankfully no bombs were dropped when I
            was there)

If you were working in the compound when Caravans or Buffalos came in, and a pouch was incoming or outgoing, someone would have to hot-foot down to the airstrip and either deliver or collect the pouch. Emails were the most common, downloaded in Nairobi and printed, flown up to Loki and out to the field locations. Outgoing emails were typed, saved on disk, and then sent to Loki and Nairobi.

On hyper-disciplined or exceptionally busy days, I could manage to put my unopened post in my tent under my pillow, and leave it until the end of the day. I think I had two of those days! Far more frequently, I'd at least have found out who each of the messages were from by the time I'd got to my tent. It was therefore almost inevitable, having got so far, to push on through, finish the job and read them! I would read, reread and re-reread any post, soaking up news from home. Doing my best to imagine the various settings and situations, I sat in my tent, trying not to let the drips of sweat running down my nose drop onto the paper.

People used to say to me, 'I don't know what to write, it all seems so boring compared with what you're doing.' That was one of the biggest fallacies out! Whether the bluebells were coming into bloom, new curtain fabric was being chosen, the car clutch had gone – I craved it all; those little ties with home, the only ones you have in the middle of the Sudanese bush. Often I would open my little photo album and take out a picture of whoever's letter I was reading. It seemed to make it all a little more personal. Feeling that sense of contact, knowing I was being thought of, missed and prayed for gave me a real sense of security.

* * * *

Sundays, as a rule, were precious. No alarm clock, the chance to lie and read, a leisurely breakfast, a few more inches of water in my bucket to wash with; church, a prayer time, lunch, 'smalls' washing, leg shaving, a walk, throwing a Frisbee around, typing emails, reading, dinner, chat, bed ... In Sudan, there isn't a lot to do leisure-wise.

Knicker-washing was a weekly event. Near the shower and the loo was an empty, upturned diesel drum. It became quite a habit for George and I to pick up a bag of neon blue 'Toss' washing powder, a few buckets, and with her sitting at that end of the drum and me sitting at this,

Sundays were for 'smalls' washing, leg shaving, a walk ...
Photo: Sarah Casey

we would soak, scrub and rinse our respective knickers, in the depths of conversation righting the world as though it were the most natural thing to do.

Because of the relatively rough treatment knickers get somewhere like Sudan, through hand washing, scrubbing and drying in the extreme sun, I wrote to – by reputation – the most popular ladies' lingerie out-fit in the UK and requested sponsorship for the programme. I commented that all the six British women on the Sudan programme were committed to their products. I explained about the lack of lingerie longevity in Sudan. I mentioned the fact that a selection of sizes 10-14 cotton 'minis' would be exceptionally well received. In due time they replied. Unfortunately, their sponsorship potential was targeted purely at UK based projects, and as such they were not in a position to be of assistance. Shame!

* * * *

There were two churches in Mike Kilo, the Pentecostal and the Episcopal.

The walls – woven grass matting or sacking sewn together.

The roof – the shade of a large tree.

The pews – wonky branches held about a foot off the ground by forked upright supports.

The altar tables – pallets from the airdrops, put together by the local carpenter.

The collection plate – a simple bag made from sacking material.

The song books – memory – songs passed from generation to generation.

The music – drums and maracas.

No stained glass windows, no padded seats, no fancy sound systems, no funky bands, no steeple to be repaired – and yet God was being worshipped, and his Gospel preached. Undoubtedly, the roofless and doorless constructions were very much houses of God.

The Episcopal church was behind our compound. Pastor Stephen led his congregation with zeal. Services were held faithfully on Sundays, weekday evenings the church would often meet, and the choir would rehearse. Drums in Sudan are a means of communicating. When the drums fall silent, it can be because of the fear of an enemy, not wanting to draw attention to a village. As a result, the sound of the drums came to mean far more to me than just music. Silent, drumless nights carried apprehension. Regardless of the volume, nights of pulsating rhythm, the swooshing tempo of the maracas and the indescribable sung worship harmonies were peaceful nights in more ways than one. They became my lullabies.

The beaming worship leader at the Pentecostal church would always bring a grin to my face. He would dance and march and shimmy and stamp and slap and sway, seemingly all at once as the church musically declared 'I'm a soldier in the army of the Lord!'

Most of the songs were not in English, and I developed a habit of either kind of 'la-ing' away, or singing English words from other songs to the tune. Some of the times of prayer I had in the churches were incredibly powerful. At times it was possible to have a translation for the sermon, other times, I'd pray or read my Bible. I learnt there that the absence of a shared language need not mean the absence of fellowship.

Work

My mission, that I'd chosen to accept with absolute blind naïveté, was responsibility for: 'the co-ordination of a seeds and tool distribution to ten thousand households in Aweil East county.' I'm intrigued how at that interview, my transferable skills package of experiences, such as managing play schemes, a touch of lecturing and donning a teddy bear suit for charity fund-raisers, led Tearfund to the conclusion that I indeed was the right girl for the job! However, they had every confidence in me, so who was I to doubt them?!

Ten thousand – that's quite a lot of households. Multiply that by five-ish family members per household, and the distribution would directly affect approximately fifty thousand people's lives. It felt like a mountain of a task, but with some assistance, it was possible to break it down:

- Seven borough-like 'payams' made up the county
- Each payam had several gols (sub-borough districts)
- Within the gols were the villages
- In the villages – the households
- In the households – our target recipients, the women

Polygamy is common in Sudan. One man can have many wives, so a household isn't necessarily headed by a man – he may be away visiting one of his other wives! The women were our 'target beneficiaries'.

At each of these levels were civil and administrative leadership strata, payam administrators, chiefs, sub-chiefs, gol leaders and village representatives. What seemed to be a lamely infra-structured hotchpotch of people was actually an incredibly functional ordered community. It worked. I hadn't envisioned this. I'd just thought about rocking up at various villages, having a bit of a bun fight to ascertain which households were most vulnerable and handing over the package. What a cocky, judgemental attitude I'd taken with me of 'we'll have to enforce our structure, our methods.'

Many of my days seemed to be spent sitting underneath trees with distinguished, pipe smoking chiefs, scratching out distribution systems in the dust with their long gnarled sticks. Their 'dress' was the jellaba, a very funky yet functional two piece number that in 1999 was available in the royalist of royal blues, racing green or off-white. Prices would vary with the quality of the fabric, the detail of the stitching, and the presence or absence of the local designer's contrasting colour tag on the chest pocket. I make no joke – labels have some mileage in the bush of Sudan.

★ ★ ★ ★

'That tree, at that place, at that time' were the classic meeting details I would be given.

'Oh – *that* tree, at *that* place', I'd knowingly respond. Not meaning to look a fool, I'd nod sagely, looking around the village at all the trees, wondering just which one 'that' one was. My wondering would become wandering as I walked from tree to tree looking for my chiefs. The trees were like boardrooms. Status dictated how close meeting attendees could sit to the trunk and therefore the best shade, and also what they would sit on. The lack of walls and doors meant all meetings were accessible to the public, although there seemed to be a strict level of protocol that ensured an observing role only for the bystanders.

'That time' – a casual flick of the head, an exaggerated eyebrow raised over a stare held at some seemingly random point above the horizon. The Sudanese are relatively unfazed by the minutes and seconds of this world. Security incidents aside, I never saw anything remotely resembling a rush, or even a hurry in Sudan. 'That time' was always a relatively flexible one. I'd often take my notebook, a sheet of airmail paper, my book, my Bible, anything to while away the inevitable wait. It was quite a mentality shift, letting go of the necessity of keeping to time. The liberation of taking off (and ultimately losing) my watch was great.

Land is tended by hand, and in some cases tilled by ox driven ploughs. This is a relatively new innovation; until recently, women have used small hand tools to tackle pretty sizeable areas. The value placed upon cattle was too high to consider using them to take on this kind of gruelling work. Pulling a plough, too demeaning for a cow – fine for a woman. Gender equity hasn't yet swept through southern Sudan, hasn't yet so much as knocked on the door.

★ ★ ★ ★

'Morning, Big Red Cow!' Relatively abusive in a UK setting, I was led to believe by John that in Sudan being called *Aluel* was quite flattering. The Dinka people of Sudan are historically pastoralists, and their cows are their health and wealth; the number of cows a man owns states his standing in society. John was Tearfund's food security man. His responsibility was to put the feeding team out of a job. His ultimate aim was to assist communities to produce or find their own food and be nutritionally sufficient again. Quite a task in Sudan, where climatic conditions and frequent displacement of the population from one area to another severely limits their ability to grow crops and successfully pasture cows.

John and I worked very closely and I considered him something of a personal guru. He was Sudanese and whatever there was to know about indigenous crops, suitable strands of rice to grow and how close to the river, soil types, harvesting and best conditions for sorghum and groundnut growth – John knew it. If he didn't know it, he had that rare quality of knowing he didn't know it, and invariably knowing someone who did. He had a smile that involved not only his mouth but his whole face, and his eyes were joyful. My respect and love for John grew, so when he issued me with my Dinka tribal name, it was quite an honour.

The majority of the tools came in from Loki. We had a spell of three days when we received seven flights. Forty-nine tonnes worth of tools – that's a lot. Pilots were usually keen to unload their freight and clear off. No fork lift trucks, no conveyor belts – this was manpower in the rawest sense. Pick up a box, pass it down the human chain and stack it in a pile, again, again and again. The lack of urgency used to rile me and my response would be to get on with it myself. Outcomes were mixed: I would become physically exhausted as I worked feverishly away. Our local staff would become massively embarrassed that the white boss was having to do such a menial task and would rush, ridiculously casually, to my assistance. The labourers, charged with unloading the flights, would be offended by the Tearfund staff doing their job – which would cause harsh words, raising the stress of the situation further. I showed a lack of cultural sensitivity and understanding. Inevitably, with or without my feisty input, the job would have been done. Another of those lessons it took a few repeat classes for me to grasp.

Another of John's cracking innovations was the 'food for seed swap'. We would exchange imported food for locally grown seeds. The benefits for us were that we knew the seeds grew well in the locality, and we had easy access to food supplies and poorer access to imported seeds. The benefit locally was much wanted food, in exchange for what, in many cases, would have been too many seeds. One of the main farmers we used was Ajou Dit. Ajou was a progressive farmer, a rich and successful man and also incredibly generous with his community. They all shared in his success, they were all fed and had opportunities to work. He even contributed to the salaries of teachers in the area to educate the children.

Ajou Dit lived one and a half hours drive from Mike Kilo in Umdraman. Logistically, it was necessary to do three round trips a day of nine hours, for four days a week for a fortnight. Sometimes a track was distinguishable through the trees and scrub, other times not. In the early days, I used to have to strain my eyes to pick out our tyre tracks from previous trips in the dust. Recognising different arrangements of bushes and distinctive features on particular trees, I felt as though my tracking instincts were becoming honed. However, many were the times my driver beside me would tut, shake his head, spit out the window (which thankfully was usually open) wave his arms and point seemingly nowhere, to nothing. I'd missed a turning. Of course I had – only a fool could have missed that there is a slight pothole, and, look, a groundnut bush on the corner; both markedly different from the other slight pothole and groundnut bush the way I had come!

Twelve hour days out and about. Conversation was minimal in the vehicle; verging on non-existent, comfortable. I used to split the driving with our driver, also called Ajou. He had wowed me at interview and the obligatory test drive, in that he knew that he needed to use the clutch to change gear. Leaps and mechanical bounds above the other applicant. Although I'd often notice that we'd been driving for a long time with the handbrake on, Ajou was meticulous in indicating. Other than one army vehicle, one other NGO vehicle and the second

Tearfund car – our pick-up was the only vehicle in the area on the road. The importance of maintaining clear, accurate signals in traffic congestion such as that in Aweil East was obviously paramount!

Ajou and I slickened up our pit-stop wheel changing routine over the weeks. Thorns grew long, sharp and as tyre-penetrating as you like. One day we managed to jack up, switch, jack down and head off for an awesome twenty seconds before having to change our second wheel. Both punctures were in the middle of the day, far from any shade; sweating at such a rate into the dry air that you're not even aware you're doing it, there isn't time for the sweat to sit on your skin, it gets evaporated. You have to get your hands dirty and get stuck in.

Doom and gloom did not descend, however, as I was later proposed to that day by Ajou Dit on behalf of his son. Two hundred and fifty cows were offered as a dowry. Though flattered, I politely declined, mumbling that I'd have to ask my dad or something similar. Ajou Dit was persistent and creatively offered two hundred and fifty cows worth of camels for my hand instead. Tempting!

The beginning of the end

Seed by seed and tool by tool, we prepared. The 8th April was our first long and eagerly awaited seeds and tools distribution date. Weeks and weeks of prep finally with some tangible output. We'd driven to the distribution site, unloaded the vehicle and were sitting discussing the plan with the chiefs, when gradually I started feeling ill, dizzy, muggy-headed and with an unsettled stomach that contained something that violently felt that it should come out, one way or the other. I made my excuses and walked away from the meeting, sat down somewhere by myself and promptly threw up.

With that, George appeared in the pick-up with the second batch of seeds and tools, looked at me, and suggested strongly that I go back to base. By this stage I was feeling less and less well, and offered little resistance. I nodded off on the way home, only to be woken on the edge of Mike Kilo by the driver nudging me. I groggily opened my eyes to see villagers running towards us, heading out of the village. Quite an instantaneously reviving tonic!

Over the next few hours, it was decided by team leaders – in accordance with the security plans – that all the Mike Kilo based NGO workers would evacuate. By now, I was trotting to the pit latrine so frequently with diarrhoea that my residency there was threatening to become secure through squatters' rights … I continued to vomit. One of the nurses on the team gave me some bug-killing tablets for the tummy which seemed to barely bounce off my stomach wall before coming straight back up. I did my best to help pack up and secure the compound. It wasn't possible for a plane to land in Mike Kilo, so we left the compound quite late in the evening to drive to an agreed point where we would overnight and be collected the next morning.

That drive was absolutely hilarious. I guess adrenaline was high in all of us, and as the two cars headed out through the bush in the dark of the night, it felt like more of a jolly than an emergency evacuation. Thankfully my diarrhoea had passed and there was nothing left to vomit. It took about four times as long as it should have to reach the airstrip and the adjoining compound that we were staying in. Exhausted, we slept.

The Buffalo plane arrived mid morning the next day to take us out. I still wasn't eating, but hadn't been sick since the previous evening. There weren't enough seats on the cargo plane, so a number of us were sprawled on the floor with various bags and blankets. The flight to Loki was uneventful, and we were met by the Tearfund logisticians on arrival. After the last two days of stressy decision making and responsibility bearing, George headed off to the beach on her scheduled R&R. In Loki they'd sorted out accommodation for us, and I slept.

The security situation in Mike Kilo calmed down over the next few days, and the clinic in Loki dosed me up with medicine. Gradually, I started feeling so much better that I managed to convince the visiting UK boss that I was well enough to go back to Mike Kilo with the team. I was so well, in fact, that twenty-four hours after arriving back, I was Medivacced back out to Loki. I had one of those unlabelled conditions that resulted in me being flown from Loki down to Nairobi hospital in an air ambulance with a drip. I was really disappointed. We'd just started the distributions and I end up in a hospital bed, hundreds of miles away, vigorously losing weight.

The Nairobi-based team were really good in visiting with magazines and flowers. Als was out of Sudan on R&R and chose to stay in Nairobi. Rest and recuperation is gold dust; you work six weeks, six days off, work six weeks … You need it, daydream about it, plan your next one before you go back in. So for Als to stay in Nairobi, faithfully visit me in hospital daily, sit reading whilst I'd sleep, chat when I was awake and bring in various treats still blows me away. One day when it seemed increasingly inevitable that 'home time' was looming, she sat on my bed, heard my frustrated woes – and cried with me. No one had ever done that and it had a profound effect on me. She shared my grief, my disappointment, my distress. That simple act spoke more loudly to me about support, about sharing my hurt, and about demonstrating love than anything anyone could have said to me at that time. Makes me wonder what effect Jesus' weeping about Lazarus' death must have had on Mary.

After the first few sleep-dominated days, I started to long to be discharged from hospital. But the weight that had fallen off so quickly over the last week, was not falling back on. I was discharged on the proviso that I did not return to Sudan until my clothes and I were a better size match. My appetite had left me, so for the next few days in Nairobi – no weight gain. I knew I wasn't well enough to go into Sudan, but desperately wanted to, and knew I should go home, get back to health and come out again. It was my first assignment, the last thing I wanted to do was have to go home. What if they didn't let me back? What if I'd been more trouble than I was worth? In the end I was told I was going home. It was the right decision, that I couldn't, or rather wouldn't make myself. I left Nairobi knowing I probably wouldn't get back in time for the rest of the distribution. But I'd been offered a contract extension in a new role working in Loki as a logistician. I left Nairobi on 20th April. I was met at Heathrow by the UK based project officer who took me to the Tropical Medicine Hospital for tests, and then got me on a flight home to Jersey. Not the most comforting of first assignments for mum and dad – insecurity, Medivacs, nothing like breaking them in gently.

Home is undoubtedly the best place to be poorly and I took seriously the task of regaining weight. All my culinary favourites were brought in; seconds and even thirds were encouraged. In two weeks I was back to my rock steady 69kg, so immediately called Tearfund UK to ask for a ticket out. I flew back out to Nairobi on 12th May, two days after the birth of my second niece, Bex. It was an incredible bonus to be around in the UK for that. My sister called from the hospital and spoke first to Kates (aged three) to tell her about her new sibling. I asked Kates what Mummy had said, and with dinner-plate eyes she excitedly looked up at me and babbled out:

'I've got a baby brother, she's called Becky!'

★ ★ ★ ★

Chuffed to bits to be back, I was settling into Loki well. My second day proved a little more eventful than anticipated. The letter below was my effort to reassure my parents.

19/05/99,

Dear All

I'm up in Loki again now, having had one night in 'the biggest war hospital in the world', and then two more in Nairobi hospital. The CT scan and EEG all clear, no sign of epilepsy – probably reaction from my malaria prophylaxis toxicity. Outcome – new malarial drug prescribed, I'm not to drive for two weeks, and have to report any 'funny turns' to the Doc. All took me a bit by surprise. I'd done a morning's work here, and was walking from my tent to the office, felt wobbly, squatted down, knew I was not right, thought about calling someone on the radio, and then next I knew was sitting with Nigel and Jane just chatting about the day. Didn't believe them when they told me what had happened, until I saw the grazes on my wrist, shoulder and chin – I had a good old roll around apparently! Then headache came, and they decided to send me out (to Nairobi), air ambulance got here at dusk and wasn't prepared to fly in the dark, so I was taken to Lopiding (hospital). Flew down to Nairobi the next morning, the rest you know.

Since then I've been feeling fine – bit concerned that that's the second one. The tests in Nairobi were as thorough as they would have been in the UK so I feel no need to come home for any treatment or anything. It was just all frustrating having just got back, etc. Getting or have got a reputation – one security evacuation, and two medivacs in five weeks with three of those weeks spent in the UK – an unenviable record! Anyway sorry to worry you again! Alison is in Loki tomorrow and George on Friday so it will be good to speak to them about it all, and just chat it through – missing having my team around me. There are so many acquaintances here, but not friends, yet!

Will write more tomorrow. Love Em XXX

There I was getting to grips with a new job, felt a little bit odd and had a seizure in the middle of Loki. I returned to the same ward in Nairobi hospital that I'd been in the month before. The tests and scans showed no abnormalities, and after a few days bed-rest the doctor confidently allowed me back up to Loki. I was there just one day and then felt those same sensations I had just before I fitted. I didn't 'fit', but knew that it wasn't appropriate for me to stay. Als walked me over to my room and I slept for a few hours. I'd started packing before she told me that I was going home. She knew how excited I was to be back, how much I wanted to be in Loki. I could see in her face the disappointment that mirrored my own. I'd just got back.

I left Kenya on 26th May.

Chapter 4

The Summer of Discontent

'So, Emma, how are you coping with your epilepsy?'

That casual little one-liner came as a bit of a shock from the doctor one month after I got back to the UK. I knew that fits and epilepsy went hand in hand, but also that people could have 'one-off fits', triggered by extreme circumstances, heat, dehydration, stress or the build up of certain drugs. That was the first time anyone had attached a label to it to me, and if it had been purely a 'one off' then diagnosing epilepsy was surely a little unnecessary. Apparently not, though.

A few years before whilst I was on my Easter jollies from Chester I'd been *en famille* in Taunton, had felt a bit light-headed and wobbly, took myself out of the shop for a bit of fresh air, and ... woke up some time later in a hospital bed, with no trousers on, being talked to by my sister! I had no idea what had happened, how I got there, nor, to my embarrassed amusement, why I had no trousers on. I felt as though it was a trick. Unfamiliar with fainting, I just could not understand this 'there one minute, here the next' phenomenon. It felt comical at the time. I don't think Mum, Dad and Sara were as unbothered by it as I was. Dad was looking at the shop window a few feet away, only to turn around and find his daughter flat out convulsing away on the ground. Mum and Sara walked out of the shop to the same spectacle.

I was treated like a princess for the rest of the day. I had to say if I was hungry, thirsty or sleepy – and food, drink and rest were immediately provided. Follow-up tests in Chester, tracing brain activity, verified that I was normal. With no obvious trigger to the fit, no abnormalities revealed, life continued as usual. The doctor explained we all could have one fit, for no apparent reason, and never have any further problems – a 'one off'. The twelve month driving ban wasn't really a problem as I didn't have a car. It took a few months to get back full confidence that it wouldn't happen again, but with no recurrence, it was a minimal disruption to my life.

The second 'one off' in 1999 understandably took me into a different category, but hearing the word 'epilepsy' took me by surprise. I left the doctor and went round to the Tearfund office in Teddington, still trying to familiarise myself with not just the label but the potential implications of it. How would people treat me? Would I be fitting frequently? Another driving ban?

Relief work – I love it, just started it, is it over? Medication – permanently?

I met with the Personnel Officer who had the unenviable yet necessary task of letting me know that, soon, I would have to come off contract. It wasn't the brightest of days for me. He didn't know me well, and yet he managed to be gentle and supportive. He understood some of my fears, my confusion, and the biggest at the time – my disappointment. The general medical opinion from the variety of doctors I'd encountered in Sudan, Kenya and the UK varied from 'You need a few months to stabilise out on the medication, and then we can look at possibilities of you going abroad again', to the more frequently stated line of 'Relief work is not suitable for epileptics.'

Disappointment was high and there was a sadness at having found what made me tick work-wise, only to be told that, because of something I had no control over, I couldn't do it.

The control factor was massive; as was the realisation of an imposed boundary that I could do nothing about. I'd been told that I needed to be sensible, work out my boundaries, and not put myself in stressful situations. My reaction wasn't of peaceful acceptance. It was motivated by two fears and fears are not the most rational of human attributes. The first was how other people might react, shrinking my boundaries further than they needed to. The second, and this was the bigger fear of the two, was selfish. It was sinking in that I had the potential to fit at any time. It was not at all likely if I was on my drugs, looking after myself, sleeping and eating well, but a seed of fear had taken root that I could fit like a Martini – any time any place. Tied to that was my fear that I would start playing safe, living life only ever reaching third gear – just in case.

There are less dramatic alternatives to coming to terms with any news like this, gradually realising what you can and can't do. But I opted for another route, not necessarily the smartest nor one I particularly endorse. I took off. I headed for the beach, the Cornish coastline. By myself. No one down there keeping an eye on me, no telephone contact. I went walking on the cliffs, swam in the sea, out of my depth, as far and as hard as I could; climbed … The doctors had suggested that if I took a bath, I did it with someone else in the house, and left the bathroom door unlocked. One month in the middle of Sudan, up to my eyeballs in work, living in a mud hut, hundreds of miles from anywhere, the next – taking a bath, with someone on standby! I couldn't live with that level of permanent fear – waiting constantly for a fit that might or might not happen. That's like looking at every person you pass on the street or car on the road and waiting for them to hit you!

I met up with Roz at Polzeath one day. She'd finished her assignment in Sudan and was just back home in Liskeard. We ate ice cream, walked along the beach and sat on the rocks. Contrary to usual form, we didn't talk much. I find it hard to articulate at times, and didn't have any words then. Those who know me well will testify that I can talk endlessly on anything that doesn't *really* matter to me. The 'big stuff' though, I'm slow in coming forward with. Those friends and family who will accept my silence, as well as enjoy my conversation are valued indeed. Rozzy sat with me in my silence as we watched the ocean.

I'm acutely aware how vague much of this period is in my mind. I seem to have developed selective recall about that time. It amazes me how we seem subliminally to filter out some of the more painful details of memories and look back with predominantly rose-tinted glasses – as though access is denied to certain files, and instead a woolly, 'all rightness' fills the gaps.

I spent the next few months in Exeter. My old housemates had a spare room, and welcomed me back in. As the summer went on, I had no further symptoms, my emotional keel evened out a little and the big issue was what to do. 'God-wise', I did not get it. Having loved the work

I was involved in, I did not understand why it had happened. I was missing my team in Sudan, missing my work, and was apathetic and clueless about what to do next. I hadn't been working for a couple of months and thin air was becoming tricky to live on. I was slowly accepting that for now, maybe not for ever, I couldn't go away with Tearfund. I prayed about it, but prayers appeared to go unanswered. Out with the jobs pages again. A friend had told me that the Christian bookshop in town was advertising for a sales person. There was nothing else that I wanted to do, so I picked up the application form, knowing that I didn't want the job. The day I completed it, I got a call from the Tearfund personnel officer: 'Would you consider going to Kosovo?'

I resisted asking 'Is the Pope Catholic?', but listened whilst he explained about the project, the location, my potential role, why he (and the Medical Advisor) didn't think it would be a problem health-wise, due to the climate, access to health facilities, living conditions etc, as long as I adhered to a set of behaviour guidelines to mitigate against the likelihood of further fits. I say I listened – the dual senses of relief and excitement swept over me fantastically. I had a second chance. Perhaps not such unanswered prayers after all!

I accepted the assignment.

Seeds and tools for distribution in Sudan
Photo: Georgina Brook

Chapter 5

Another Chance

Getting to know you, getting to know the people around you

Five of us flew out together from Teddington on 3rd September 1999; two going into Kukes northern Albania – Ben and Sarah (Sa); Percy, Nick and I working in Gjakove, Kosovo. We'd all been together for briefings in the office before we left and had stayed in the Tearfund flat and were getting on well. Meeting new team mates is interesting, very Big Brotherish – random strangers chosen to spend the next x weeks/months living and working in close proximity. A huge challenge for the personnel people: if it works, of course it should – no appreciation for a job well done. If it doesn't – obviously their fault for putting the wrong people together!

Briefings are great. It's like cramming frantically for exams that you've never studied for in the first place!

- Region, country and local background – programme and project orientation
- Details about your role – working environment
- Policies
- Contracts
- Accounts
- Medical
- Payroll

So it goes on, just as you're realising how many loose ends you haven't quite tied up, you're trying to do your goodbyes over the telephone and it's prep time! Bundles of paperwork, wads of information, tickets, money, visas, and when you're ready for a couple of days' breather to take it all in – you fly!

We went into Kosovo via Rome and flew into Pristina the next day. I sat next to Sa and conversation with this new colleague flowed; unhindered by the plane engines, we shouted at one another all the way into Kosovo! It was good to find a friend so early on, someone that trust and communication came quickly with. We were met at the airport by Arsim from Gjakove and Afrim from Kukes. It was just a couple of months after the major Serbian retreat from Kosovo, and as we journeyed from Pristina to Prizren it was obvious that no one had started to repair the damage. Many of the houses along the roadsides had suffered from fire. Some were partially roofless, others completely so. Many were doorless and windowless. Internal walls had fallen, external walls of buildings were peppered with scars from arms fire and the roads pitted with potholes.

I wrote home:

Six days ago I was building sandcastles on a Jersey beach on Katy's birthday, now it's Sunday afternoon here in Kosovo and I've just been for a walk along a nearby lake with some of the guys, not too far, a mine-field blocked our course. Everywhere you look you can see damage caused to a country not so dissimilar from home. On the way from Pristina airport to our base yesterday we were diverted around Prizren because an unexploded bomb had been found. Although the fighting is over, casualties or collateral damage continues.

I find it hard not to compare here with Sudan, but though the people are generally fed, clothed and watered – the trauma they have gone through in recent months, and their fall from grace has had a devastating effect on lives here. In church this morning individuals were going forward to pray for the 1500 people (mainly men) of Gjakove who are missing – possibly prisoners of war, possibly dead. People speak of brothers, fathers or sons who are missing – lives have really been ripped apart.

Our job as a team is reconstruction of homes and shelters – the aim to provide materials for villagers to repair at least one room of their house to make it fit for winter – winterisation. I'm a logistician out here for five months, working in a team of nine ex-pats – builders, engineers, etc. There is (again) an excellent atmosphere in the team here, a lot of motivation and commitment to do this work well. It's funny, I was speaking with a very good friend just before I came out here about the highs and lows of the last few months, and having been given something of a second chance at relief work feels like a real privilege. I really feel that this situation is one that God has led me to and just want to get stuck in and do it – love it!

As the letter said, I found direct comparisons with Sudan easy. The lives of the villagers in Mike Kilo were still under threat, bombs still fell, raids claimed lives, disease was rife, malnutrition affected families, and peace

The 'missing men' of Gjakove

Photo: David Sterry

hadn't been reached. Water was scarce, food limited, livelihoods were – for most – purely the daily business of staying alive. My last memories of Mike Kilo were built on three months of living alongside and in the community. I knew people and I was known. I knew some of what was going on in their lives, where they lived, who their families were. The people of Kosovo? Through those lenses? Different end of the scale. It took a long time for me to be happy with the fact that these people might need some response from the west, from Tearfund, from me, to the disaster they had faced – that it had indeed been a disaster.

I was aware that early on I was looking at properties rather than homes. That was until I started building relationships with individuals. Before that I'd merely witnessed the destruction that I was too detached from to care deeply about. It confused me that so much seemingly senseless damage had occurred. The extent and scale surprised me, but there were no feelings of involvement initially.

Work

Balkans winters are severe. Often temperatures drop below freezing for considerable lengths of time. The rush was to distribute materials to be used in emergency work to make them habitable. Initially, for the most part this involved the provision of roof materials, windows and doors.

My role was logistics; sourcing materials, purchasing, storing, and distributing them as and when required. Glorified shopping really! Prior to arriving in Kosovo I had dabbled with Meccano but I recognised that my credentials to be an integral part of a large scale construction project were relatively scant. The lingo was essential; not so much the Albanian but the construction terms, not common terminology. I progressed from 'doors and windows' to 'openings' and even 'apertures'. Although I didn't need to know an awful lot about the details of the construction process, rudimentary knowledge certainly helped. Cement and bricks – you'd think that that would be kind of adequate to get a wall up, but there were pages and pages of material lists.

The logs team for most of the project was four strong: the logistical co-ordinator who had programme-wide responsibility for co-ordination of all things logistical, two of us expat project logisticians based in Gjakove, and the renowned Milot, a Gjakoven. Milot knew everyone, and everyone knew him. He was related to most of the town. As so many projects seem to be, much of the success of this one was down to the quality and commitment of the local staff.

Gjakove was one of two project sites, Kukes in northern Albania was the second. Kukes is just a few kilometres from the border with Kosovo, and was the town that over three hundred thousand Kosovo-Albanians fled to during the dramatic exodus from Kosovo as a result of the conflict. The town had been overwhelmed by the influx of temporary inhabitants. Refugee camps had sprung up. The town's population multiplied. Tearfund had worked there during this immediate crisis time in the glamorous role of water and sanitation work. Toilets and waste disposal were our forte. Not pretty but an essential role.

Once the Serbs retreated from Kosovo, the Kosovo-Albanians returned to it, almost as swiftly as they had fled. As the refugees left Kukes, the NGOs left with them and the capacity that NGO money can buy left too. Kukes fell from the limelight. Tearfund – with the other NGOs – was not slow in crossing the border into Kosovo, keen to assess the needs of the returning refugees and witness the extent of the damage and devastation they were going home to find. Tearfund also – with conspicuously few other NGOs – chose to maintain an active presence in Kukes; a decision acknowledged with gratitude by the community of Kukes in the presentation of a special award of appreciation to the organisation. By September, specific projects were in place to help rehabilitate the town.

The project sites of Gjakove and Kukes were serviced by the geographically central programme office in Prizren, staffed by two national team members and two expats; Sam the programme director and Gill the programme support officer. I love them both. I respect them professionally for the skills they brought to the programme and admire who they are beyond their job titles. Philip Yancey, seeking out a 'faith that works' commented

> As I think about individual Christians I know, I see some people made
> incomparably better by their faith, and some made immeasurably worse.
> For every gracious, kind-spirited, forgiving Christian, I can point to a
> proud, mean-spirited, judgemental one. In my own experience, those
> who strive the hardest and believe the most fervently are some of the
> least attractive persons. Like the Pharisees of Jesus' day, they get caught up
> in competition and end up self-righteous rather than righteous.[1]

Since I became a Christian, I have been more aware of a judgemental
thread within me in than I'm happy to admit. But some Christians do
seem to get it more right. Sam and Gill seemed to possess the rare combination of qualities that blends reality and humanity with a deep level
of faith and commitment.

Team Gjakove – a biggish team: I think we peaked at a substantial
twelve. Contracts varied in length according to people's availability and
the role that they were employed to fill, so there was always a regular
turnover of people.

Dave was already out there when I arrived, and became my closest
buddy. There are a lot of similarities between us; we can laugh at the
same things, be interested in similar stuff, enjoy time spent together,
and understand each other well. On the other hand though, Dave is
an antidote to some of my significant weaknesses, having patience
beyond comprehension when mine has run dry long ago, and wisdom
that my thinking does not allow me to reach. He adds an edge of pru-
dent caution to my more impulsive moments, is gentle when my
tongue lashes out inconsiderately, faithful when my faith wanders, and
humble when my pride stands tall. I learnt a lot from Dave and grew
to value his friendship massively. Many were the tears, the laughs, the
prayers, the harsh words, the conversations and the silences we shared.
And still do.

★ ★ ★ ★

Within my first couple of weeks we were expecting two generators, or
'gennies' into Pristina. Having heard that they were quite substantial

---

[1] P. Yancey, *Soul Survivor* (London: Hodder & Stoughton, 2001) p116

pieces of machinery, I arranged for one of our Bedford trucks to go and collect them rather than one of the Land Cruisers. I'd sorted out a driver – all ready to roll. I'd even had the insight to send the truck with the hoist. It transpired later that the two 'gennies' arriving in Pristina were in fact two 'Jennies' – two members of UK-based Tearfund staff, on a visit to the region, both called Jenny. Collected the next day in a Land Cruiser, they were swiftly informed by my team-mates that they should consider themselves lucky they weren't crated, hoisted and lashed on to the bed of a truck for the journey. Great to leave your professional mark early on with these things.

My room and its view

The view out of my bedroom window was across the suburbs of Gjakove. The view wasn't unpleasant. Houses in the Balkans are big, with a lot of big rooms in each house. I learnt quickly that the phrase 'An Englishman's home is his castle' is probably even more apt in the Balkans. Banking is not trusted. Banks have gone bust, swallowing more than individuals could afford to lose. Houses? That's where to put your money. Knit this with a strong sense of family and extended family, and inevitably houses are substantial. Houses are a mark of family standing in the community, of security. When there is money available you build a bit more, perhaps the brickwork of another level. More money some time later? Add doors and windows – or plastering, electrical installations. Over time, the house grows. Imagine that instead of setting up any investments, you plough that money into your house. Instead of a pension – much of it goes into your house. Imagine then that this home is torched. All your eggs, in the one basket – smashed. The majority of what you have, what your parents and their parents worked for, has gone. I cannot overstate the importance a home carried in Kosovo. The consequences of losing one were manifold and profound.

In September, out of my window I could see as many charred timber roof frames, naked without their tiles, as I could see complete roofs; as many unfilled rectangular gaps as glazed windows; as many facades

peppered with the dot to dot markings of gun fire as unriddled buildings. The physical damage had not yet been undone.

Beyond the chaos of the roof tops were a low range of foothills, and
above them, mountains. Every morning, there were the mountains.
Every evening – there the mountains still were. Whatever was happening in the foreground, whatever state the suburbs were in, the
mountains didn't change. They were stable. I was struck often by the
parallels between that picture and the view I have of my world. So often
I get bogged down in the messiness of the foreground, rather than lifting my eyes up to the mountains.

Gjakove

Gjakove was a beautiful town. Tucked away behind the more modern
urban developments was the old town. Narrow, cobbled streets, low
level buildings, mews with hidden courtyards behind vast wooden gates
maintaining their legacy and secrets. Small shops, businesses, cafes,
restaurants, bars, homes – the pulse to which the rest of the town held
fast. Glass and chrome cafés nestled amidst more traditional tailoring
shops. It felt as though it were the real hub of the town, that which had
lasted time and would not be beaten by it.

It was this part of Gjakove that seemed particularly targeted during
the conflict. Building after building succumbed to fire. Now it lay in
ruins. It struck me as odd initially that this relatively economically val-
ueless part of the town was picked out, that this quirky little area should
be the most damaged. But it was the heart of the town. It was one of
the cruellest blows that could be dealt. Areas of industry, finance or
commerce could have been destroyed without causing such emotional
loss. But the hub of heritage ... that got Gjakove where it hurt.

I got ridiculously excited about the possibility of regenerating the
rows of shops that looked down on the market square. Milot had managed to acquire architectural plans, and the vision of that part of town
up and swinging again took little imagination. The issue got a little
fogged though when compared with the slightly more pressing task of

winterising homes. Obstacles such as land ownership, store ownership, loans or grants further muddied the waters. The minor detail of whether café refurbishment fulfilled DRT's then mandate (now adapted) 'to reduce the death and suffering of vulnerable people through operational relief responses to major disasters' was questionable.

We didn't regenerate the market place – a right decision. But I still wonder, in terms of recovery, whether money spent there – though it might not have reduced death and suffering – would have had significant impact on life.

★ ★ ★ ★

By the time I arrived in September, a wall had been built of light grey bricks backing on to a small park near the Civic Centre. There were fifteen hundred bricks in the wall. On each brick was a name, written in thick black marker pen. Every week on Sunday evening a group could be seen standing in a circle on the steps of the Civic Centre. Often holding hands, sometimes they'd sing. Whatever the weather, they'd be there, for about thirty minutes or so, some speaking in Albanian, others in English. Heads bowed, tears would often flow, sobs audible at times. The names on the bricks were of the missing men in Gjakove. The group of people in the circle were relatives or friends, led in prayer by the local evangelical church.

My attendance at this weekly meeting varied. Initially, I was expecting the release of the men and their return to Gjakove. I assumed it would happen – fighting was over. Then my assuredness wavered. It wasn't definite that they were alive. 'Missing' didn't just mean 'captured by the Serbs and held in prison', 'missing' potentially encompassed the dead as well; those who had been shot, yet confirmatory evidence was not available. It became increasingly unlikely that all the men would be coming home. I didn't know how to pray.

To pray boldly in faith for their release when so many might be dead already seemed to offer almost a cruel thread to those awaiting their return. To admit that they might be dead seemed faithless. I could tie myself up in knots about it. I felt angry that the church seemed to be petitioning the Lord so strongly for the men's release, whilst I felt this nagging sense that this was not possible. I'd then feel guilty if I prayed for acceptance, for comfort, for ability for those left behind to move on. The 'Your will be done' prayer seemed to miss the mark. Often my thoughts would just quieten, my prayer would be the questions rather than any answers.

10/10/99

One stretch of road we needed for our work had a blockade set up on it by local people. It was impassable. The alternative was a tedious three hour diversion. The reason the blockade was there was to prevent Russian peace-keeping forces being deployed in the area. During the height of the conflict, Russian soldiers who had not been paid at home would allegedly put on Serb military uniforms, and act as mercenaries supporting the Serb efforts. One night, during the last Serb offensive in that area, a village lost hundreds of its people in a massacre. Throughout the attack, Russian-speaking soldiers were heard alongside the Serbs. The community was understandably incensed at the prospect of the Russians returning. The local people set up an impenetrable block, sealing off all access to the villages beyond that had suffered during this horrific offensive.

An extract from a letter home:

I bumbled up to this blockade, and asked to speak to whoever was in charge, to negotiate to get some of our trucks through. I understood why they wouldn't let the Russians in, but I'm not Russian, I'm English and we are trying to shift humanitarian aid – totally reasonable and rational argument. This guy X listened, and then started talking– he's a teacher, six of his class were killed (8, 9 and 10 year olds), his father had his eyes cut out, and then his head cut off (old man maybe 70ish). One family lost nine members, an eight year old girl and her Granddad remain alive. As he was telling me this, tears were pouring down his cheeks, he lost his balance and needed to be supported by his friends. His left arm came out of his pocket, missing a hand. 'They' had cut it off. He was about my Dad's age, an educated and prominent, dignified man, who couldn't stand

and could hardly speak because of his grief. What amazed and shocked me though, he didn't talk of revenge, he saw the blockade as a means of preventing more bloodshed, more lives lost.

He has enough love inside him still – just – to not seek revenge, and that just blows me away. Amidst all the evil of war, all the truly outrageous atrocities that have been committed, all the grief, there is still love. Hate has not consumed this man – incredible. X is coming for coffee next week, because he wants to talk, he needs people to know what's gone on. In the meantime, a three hour diversion for our trucks has suddenly become a whole lot more acceptable!

The arrogance of the girl! I strode up to this man, shamefully self-righteous, miffed at the lack of consideration these people were showing for other people 'trying to get on with their jobs and help sort out some of this mess.' I cringe as I look back on my attitudes to what I saw as a logistical problem. I was sure that my negotiation skills would come to fruition as we discussed the merits of lifting the road block to ensure our humanitarian aid could get where we wanted it three hours sooner. It had not crossed my mind that the blockers were not merely trying to prove an awkward political point; that their reason for blocking the road might be more important than my desire to have it unblocked.

I learned a big lesson that day. Thankfully X had had the patience to deal with me. I left the village that afternoon feeling exhausted; disappointed at my lack of sensitivity, and appalled by the atrocities that I had heard about. I was frightened by the way – if I were that man – I might react in his situation, though strangely encouraged by the absence of talk of reprisals. I remember being driven back to Gjakove and the almost tangible presence of the 'I told you so' of the local team member driving our vehicle who had tried to talk me out of confronting the blockers. As we sat silently together on the drive home, I didn't quite have the grace to tell him I'd been wrong. We went around the blockade after that.

* * * *

I found it an interesting challenge to try and keep Kates and Bex up to speed on what I was doing. I was keen to take on full responsibility for enlarging their young horizons and offering them as clear a picture as possible of the goings on in the Balkans.

Dear Katy and Becky,

I had a big work problem this week. In the summer one country called Serbia tried to be in charge of a place called Kosovo, but the people in Kosovo didn't want that, so Serbia and Kosovo started fighting. Serbia burnt some of Kosovo's houses. When the fighting stopped lots of the houses had no roofs. That's what we're here to do – to put new roofs on the broken houses.

Serbia make very good roof tiles and one of the men I'm working with bought some. But at the moment Kosovo and Serbia aren't friends, so I had to cancel the order because the Kosovo people would be upset if they had to put Serbian tiles on their roofs. We had to buy our tiles from a different country and it will take longer for them to come. It was a very difficult decision – to use tiles from people the Kosovo people don't like at the moment or to leave them in the cold and wet with no roof for longer and wait and get the tiles from their friends' country.

Love you both – more than you know
Aunty Em XXXXX

Political commentary to three year olds is not an easy task. I think with the gap-filling efforts of Sara and Andy, Kates got the gist.

I found the roof tile issue to be quite an ethical scruple. We'd heard of NGOs providing and installing Serbian manufactured materials in another region of Kosovo, only for the homes to be destroyed by the owners. Kosovo-Albanians did not want Serbian materials. We knew that receiving tiles from Italy or Montenegro, which realistically were our alternatives, could result in delays of three weeks. We knew that at this stage – November – three weeks could see us well into winter.

We knew too, though, that to go ahead and supply the Serbian tiles could result in the same problems as experienced elsewhere. An alternative non-Serbian order was placed for the tiles not yet on the road. Members of the national team chatted to community leaders who assured them that they would be far happier with the already-ordered tiles, from anywhere, rather than wait and be without. Sterling work by the national team once again put out that potential fire.

R&R

I don't feel I'd really made the most of it in Sudan. Though the bed was very comfortable, the staff hospitable and the quality of the food highly palatable; compared with the possibilities of Zanzibar, Lamu, Mount Kenya and the game reserves, the hospital in Nairobi just wasn't what I'd hoped for. The pressure was on in Kosovo to use this fantastic privilege a little more creatively.

Italy it was. Sa, Dave and I had negotiated with our respective project co-ordinators to take our breaks at the same time. Four of us flew from Pristina to Rome. The fourth was Nick. He was on his way home to coincide with his daughter's half term and was an excited man. We stayed in Rome for the night; Dave, Sa and I planning to hire a car the next day and head vaguely in the direction of Tuscany, and Nick awaiting his onward flight to the UK. The four of us ate together that evening, and sat outside in the hotel courtyard chatting late into the night. It was one of those unhurried chats that somehow you rarely get to have during your working week, where the topics roll and flow effortlessly like water. We sat enjoying the warmth of the Mediterranean climate. Someone suggested we pray. I don't remember any of the prayers, but I remember the depth of the commitment each of us seemed to have that night. Someone said a final 'Amen', and people seemed to appear as though on cue, the quietness lost. We parted the next morning. Nick flew home. We drove north.

The three of us had an excellent time. Three active people surprisingly adopting a pace of life not dissimilar from a Saga holiday.

We enjoyed the stunning scenery of Tuscany in the autumn, the lake-side delights of Viterbo, the unspoilt splendour of Sienna, the fragrant bouquet of the famous bottled and corked product of the Chianti region, the hidden villages we stumbled across tucked away in the hills. Language was no barrier – due entirely to the linguistic skills of the Italians. The few words we did string together we endeavoured to artic-ulate with such gusto and flourish that any shadows of doubt regarding the presence of Italian blood in our veins – cast by our grossly limited vocabulary, and non-existent grammatical skills – were swept away. The most stressful decisions of the day usually involved the food menu, and my blood pressure lowered perceptibly over the week. It was a fantastic week – one of the best.

Nick and Kevin – 12/11/99

I rushed up the stairs outside the house that Friday afternoon, charged in and saw Annie in the hall. 'Is he back yet?'

Nick was coming back out. Before he'd left a few weeks earlier for his break at home he'd offered to get me a jacket like his. It was a fan-tastic coat – reversible, fleecy on one side, waterproof on the other. I was excited about getting it, and had even found a valid excuse two days earlier to call him to see how he was and check that he had the coat! As soon as I saw Annie's face, it was obvious something was not right. 'No, Emma, he's not back', she said. My first thought was that there had been an accident on the road from the airport to Gjakove, and that he was delayed, or at worst injured. Most of the rest of the team arrived back at the house soon after me, and the atmosphere became taut. As soon as the last one was back in, we were all asked into the lounge.

'Nick and Kevin's flight has gone missing.'

Kevin, another Tearfund team member, was coming out to start work in Prizren. I didn't know him.

It didn't mean all that much to me instantly. I didn't consider exactly how an aeroplane goes missing, my mind didn't jump to any particular conclusion. It seemed possible that tracking equipment might fail.

Perhaps an emergency landing had been necessary. Bad information from the airport maybe? By early evening we were told that a crash had been confirmed. The plane had come down. Amidst the jumble of my thoughts, and how the guys might have fared, that jacket of mine and some post that they were bringing out crossed my mind.

There was still a chance though. There was confusion as to whether the crash had occurred in a mined area. It seemed that rescue efforts were being held up whilst this was established. It hadn't yet been confirmed whether or not there were any survivors. Nick was fit. He was strong, level-headed. If anyone was going to step out of a plane crash alive, it was going to be him. In my thoughts at that time, Nick was still alive. Until there was no chance, there was still a chance.

Soon afterwards it was confirmed that there were no survivors. I called my parents. I didn't know what to say. I just wanted them to hear my voice and know I wasn't on that flight, to know I was alive. The crash had been on the News at home – they'd seen it. Staff in Tearfund UK had spoken with them – they knew what had happened. We didn't speak for long – little to say, and little to hear.

The team members were each hit differently by the news of Nick and Kevin's deaths. Emotions came at different times, in different ways; disbelief, walking off, anger, weeping, wanting company and comfort. We were due out for Bekim's birthday bash that Friday evening. One by one the national staff arrived at the house. One by one we shared the news with them. Bekim had worked with Nick for the six weeks before he had gone home. All day every day they had been together. He'd been looking forward to Nick arriving back in Gjakove in time to join his birthday celebrations. Now he was being told Nick was dead. Gradually the news was spread.

One of the national team I told filled up instantly. An instant flow of tears that seemed to vanish as quickly as it had arrived. Tears were replaced by anger. Replaced by rage. 'This should not happen to you.' He drew a controlled breath and carried on. 'You have come out to help us. You should not die here. It is wrong. It is wrong.'

The next morning I was at the warehouse. The team of labourers and drivers were usually high-spirited. We told the men the news. They wept.

Dave was in the UK. I called him.

'You've heard the news?'

'Yeah.'

'How are you doing?'

The line went quiet. It stayed that way for moments that stretched into minutes. There was nothing uncomfortable about the silence. I didn't have the slightest desire to put down the phone in the absence of words from either of us. It was the closest we could get from where we were. Words would have just crowded that closeness.

The news and repercussions were gradually sinking in. I knew what had happened, what it meant. But there was a gap in thoughts becoming feelings. It took me a long time really to grieve for their deaths, about three months.

By Sunday afternoon, I needed to get out. The atmosphere in the house was difficult. It couldn't not be. There were about eight of us in the team then, each dealing with the loss in our own ways. I needed a change of scene. I needed some space. Annie and I drove down to Prizren. The team from Kukes had come over, and it was good to be able to spend some time chatting with Sa and the others.

Tearfund UK had sprung into action. Teddington-based colleagues were on their way out; some to Pristina where Paul and Sam were still dealing with the aftermath; others accompanying Nick and Kevin's relatives; still more on their way to us. Just as my respect and appreciation for not only what Tearfund does, but also what Tearfund is had risen during the times of insecurity and bad health I'd had in Sudan, so it soared again as they responded to this tragic loss.

Two people came to Gjakove; Liz, one of the personnel officers and Ian, the international operations director. What a time to walk into a group of people. They did a great job. Within the Tearfund hierarchy, Ian was effectively my boss's, boss's, boss's, boss's boss. They were available to chat, to be there with us and for us. The most striking memory I have of their visit is of Ian getting on with the dishes, again and again. It's funny how that has stuck with me; not the way he spoke with us as a group, not the chat I had with him at some point during his stay, but the strongest message of love and support that he gave was in his coming alongside, mucking in, and being with us in the mundane bits of those horrific days.

14/11/99

Dear All,

Morning. Today is the day that Nick and Kevin's families have to ID their bodies – I still don't really feel that it's sunk in, we've seen the pictures, we've read the reports, we've heard the details, but it is just so hard to understand that …

OK – it's Tuesday night now. Things here have really moved on – guys from Teddington flew out on Saturday and have really been supporting us, and it is great to feel part of a big family of Tearfund that has shown its love over the last few days. I've had to tell a lot of people about Nick's death, national staff, warehouse staff, etc and their response has been amazing. It's a very rare thing to meet a man who people can only say good things about. Crying out here for men is a bit of a no no, but guys have just been breaking down with the news, a real testimony to a man who I feel privileged to call my team-mate, my friend and my brother……… My heart is aching for his family and what they must be going through. This is the first death of anyone close to me since I became a Christian, and I really expected my faith to be stretched and tested – but I can say 100% that I know Nick is now in heaven, with the loving God he spent his life serving and that just blows me away. The tragedy has brought the team so much closer – it couldn't not. At different times in different ways people are grieving. As for me, I'm still waiting for the tears, they're not here yet, but I know they'll come. Nick's death feels as though part of our body has been lost, a hand cut off, we're not quite complete. But I know wounds heal; scars remain, but wounds do heal.

I want to thank you all for your emails, phone calls, prayers, love and support – even though we're miles apart, I feel very close, very loved and very held right now. We're having a thanksgiving service tomorrow, and I'm leading worship – imagine! Thankfully, the criteria of quality God uses are our hearts, not our harmonies!

I'll be in touch again soon, in the mean time love you and thank you,
God Bless, EmXXX

We'd made the decision to work on Monday, though time out was offered. On Wednesday afternoon, the whole Tearfund Balkans team met in Prizren for a service of thanksgiving. All expat and national staff, about forty of us. Some led prayers, others worship, some spoke about Nick and Kevin – it was possibly the time when we as a team became closest.

Sam spoke on Wednesday and again in Gjakove on Friday afternoon at an inter-agency service. He quoted Jim Elliot, a missionary to Ecuador who had, in the course of his work, lost his life: 'He is no fool who gives what he cannot keep to gain what he cannot lose.'

It seemed 'fine' that Nick and Kevin through their deaths had gained 'what they could not lose'. I could deal with that. It did not seem fine that those who loved them had lost them. That for me was the tragedy. None of us stand alone, we are all linked – as though on some kind of web – to other people, and an action that affects us invariably shakes the web.

Chapter 6

Seasons of Changes

Millennium

Determined to say a spectacular farewell to the twentieth century and magnificently herald in the twenty-first, stops were pulled out, hair let down, and … we played Pictionary! We did a bit more than that, but that part of the evening and the disputes that arose over 'cheating' were memorable.

The word on the card was 'wrong', someone had to draw 'wrong' as a picture.

The picture drawn was: X

It was guessed in one. Absolute anarchy broke out:

'You're cheating, you know the cards, you told him what it was, you mouthed the words to him, there is NO WAY that from a cross, you could guess "wrong". I'm not playing.'

We played the games after dinner, which was an event in itself. We hadn't quite twigged that on this auspicious night in history, restaurants might either be closed or fully booked. Having tried a number of our favourite, and indeed our less favourite haunts, we drove home resigned to rustling up 'a little something' from the packet of noodles, six oranges, tub of margarine, two sachets of soup, and tin of custard powder in the cupboard at home. Thankfully, a pizza restaurant just round the corner from the house had its lights on. We walked up the stairs – no customers, no anybody. Closed. On the way back down, we saw the owner. Obviously touched by our despondent faces, he said: 'Take a seat'. He opened the place for us!

Naturally, the 'closed' restaurant was relatively short-staffed. One of our team cued up the stereo, and played DJ for the evening. It was quite a small bar and co-bar steward Dave and I did struggle with some of the complex manoeuvres involved: opening cartons of juice, and finding glasses in the dim candle-light. For most of the meal it was just our group, the owner and the chef in the building, but as the evening went on, the place began to fill. Quality hospitality.

Home for Pictionary and then four of us wandered up to town. Town was kicking. The main street was closed to traffic and the pedestrians of Gjakove were promenading in carnival atmosphere. One of the local members of staff lived just off the high street, and in very high spirits, Elaine, Dave, Paul and I climbed the stairs to his family's apartment and knocked on the door. 'HAPPY NEW YEAR – NEARLY!' we chorused.

It was as though two worlds were separated by that door. Inside was quiet, no laughter, no joy, no excitement. Stupid of us. Blindly insensitive. This time last year there were three adult children celebrating together with their family. This year – just two. One was missing. The youngest son was absent. Captured by the Serbs? Dead? Alive?

We apologised for our intrusion, chatted a while, left and carried on quietly. At the top of town we got to the wall of bricks. We stopped and prayed together – for the missing men, their families and peace. We could hear the countdown to midnight, and simultaneously as 'Amen' was said the cheers burst forth, our tension shed, and we 'popped' our party poppers with some children. Their sound was drowned out by the rounds of small arms fire and bangers exploding around us. Italian troops were on duty in town and came under a barrage of relentless attack. They were totally ill equipped to defend themselves. The snowballs rained in on them thick and fast.

Arm in arm, we wandered back down the main street greeting people we knew – and those we didn't know – with our newly acquired Albanian phrase 'Happy New Year'. We agreed that it would be highly appropriate to head out to the nearby lake at dawn. It was a good idea, and four hours sleep is cool, it wasn't really all that cold, just a 'few below', and the odds weren't on that we'd have the same chance to herald in the next millennium! It was a beautiful start to the day – a delicate, soft pink glow in the sky that seemed to grow stronger almost before our eyes.

Winter

As winter approached, so did the end of the first phase of work. All materials had been distributed, and the majority installed. As the weather worsened, so the focus of our days changed to a monitoring role. We'd all moved from summer cottons through our wardrobes towards thermals, yet there was a dogged resistance from some to wearing the warmest of their cold weather gear. One morning in the multiple minuses, I walked with Paul who was looking rather scantily clad beside me in my layers of thermals, resembling an overdressed Guy Fawkes guy. My eyelashes had frozen, my internal nasal liquid likewise, and I asked why he just had the one pair of gloves on.

A Tearfund Distribution Centre in Kosovo
Photo: David Sterry

'I'm waiting till it gets really cold.'

As far as I was concerned, we were really cold enough to warrant wearing everything that we possibly could!

It wasn't just our clothing that kept us warm. There is evidence in photo albums that many of us accidentally adopted a blubber-like winter insulation beneath our skin. The family we were living with were supremely hospitable. Each evening, regardless of the size of our team, we would be 'cooked for'. Five days a week or so, we'd eat red meat. On that kind of diet, with diddley squat exercise, who wouldn't become slightly 'more big'! We look shocking in any snaps taken over winter, all jowelly and tubby.

Dave and I made a trip up to Pristina one weekend in winter. We were only about fifty minutes or so away from Pristina when we drove into fog, so thick we could almost feel the impact as we hit it. Dave slowed down, put on the fog light, and on we went. Visibility grew so poor that we dropped down to second gear. Conversation paused as we stared out of the windscreen for other traffic and the road! It was really cold outside so we were keen not to stop if we could possibly help it. I ended up digging out my torch and walking in front of the vehicle with my right foot on the edge of the road, holding the torch by my left hip pointing backwards. At walking pace, Dave rolled on. If I walked more than three metres in front of the vehicle, Dave couldn't see me, or the light from my torch. Fog isn't frightening – until you're in it. I could not see a thing other than the ground on which I stood. I had my radio with me, and the two of us talked through the twenty minutes I was out of the vehicle. Of all times and places, what better opportunity to discuss potential colour tones for Dave's new kitchen!

* * * *

The power supply in Kosovo had been heavily damaged during the conflict and as temperatures decreased, demand naturally increased. We had a generator which allowed us to work, most of the time. Heating was less of a certainty and it often felt as though it was colder inside than outside. The gas heaters in Gjakove left heady fumes. The electric heaters – obviously supply dependent – did not pack the necessary punch. The storage heaters could be unpredictable. When they were not working they seemed to suck in what heat a room possessed. When they worked they were fantastic and many were the times individuals could be found sitting or lying on them; on backs or on tummies, with legs and arms hanging sloth-like over their sides to hug as much warmth as possible. I tended to avoid excessive exposure of skin to the chilly air at bed time by stripping off my top half of clothes (at times four layers) all at once, rather than layer by layer. I'd then leave the cocoon of clothing on the storage heater, hopefully to be warmed by morning. Sometimes it worked, other times it didn't.

Days were short, and evenings decidedly long. Exciting as snow was for those first few days, that child-like enthusiasm to play out in it wore off quickly when it sludged up, iced over, and darkness would fall before the afternoons had run their course. We had a few games, a couple of decks of cards, newspapers were available, books, email access, etc, and for evenings with electricity the video store up the road was open. Quality was variable and we watched many real suspense thrillers. Much of the suspense came as a result of the tape cutting out part way through, and the thrilling 'choose your own adventure' creativity needed to propose a suitable ending.

As friendships deepened and we got to know each other, we tried to take better care of one another. Taking yourself out for a treat wasn't easy, so creativity was needed in terms of pampering. Foot massages and face packs seemed to go a long way to soothing away the niggliest of stresses, clearing work-focused minds. As Sa and I frequently assured Dave, many men moisturise their skin and would relish the opportunity to enjoy a face pack occasionally. The affordable yet decadent nature of these products worked wonders. I have an endearing memory of an evening Sa, Dave and I had with Sam and Gill. Having evicted them from their home, the three of us prepared dinner for them, we ate together and whilst Dave washed up, Sa and I sat at Sam and Gill's feet massaging away whilst they rested on the couch in a warm, candle-lit room each with a glass of something medicinal whilst wearing 'revitalising eye pads'. Brilliant.

Spring

The Kukes project office had closed down over winter. The next phase involving a lot of outside work on the landfill rubbish site would be restarted once the weather improved. Over winter, my job had changed and I had become the logistical co-ordinator. Although I remained Gjakove-based, my remit had broadened geographically.

The Kukes restart was scheduled for the start of March, and I was involved in kitting out the new office in preparation for the team arriving. Gill had found the place, sorted the details of contracts and the theory was that the team would be able to hit the ground running, with all those little jobs done, like plugs wired, batteries charged and ink cartridges installed. I had a great few days in Kukes with Jeremy from head office and Bekim. It's interesting that in teams individuals are included for specific reasons. Bekim provided a much needed degree of local knowledge and translation skills. Jeremy rivals 007's 'Q' in terms of technical know-how, and the skills to make it happen. It's hard to say exactly what my special contribution was but we had metamorphosed one floor into a twenty-first century, all-singing, all-dancing project office.

We were trying to set up their base station radio one day, which involved nipping up a sixish storey building to attach one end of the antenna and scrambling across a roof lower down to pick up the other end before attaching that on the office roof. Fine in normal circumstances but the trickiness was exacerbated by the inclement weather. There's rarely a good time to hang about holding a sixty-foot long antenna cable, but as the thunder clapped and the lightning began to streak, it seemed to be a decidedly bad time!

★ ★ ★ ★

Moving in and out of Kukes from Kosovo involved crossing the Morine International border. It was a wonderful border. Some days as our vehicles approached we would cheerily be waved forward to the front of the queue, other days we would less cheerily be waved back. At times, they searched our vehicles methodically and thoroughly, meticulously going through paperwork, other days they didn't check our passports. On one occasion we had three Tearfund vehicles leaving Albania for Kosovo, and we happened to have three girls in the lead vehicle. The other two vehicles had the guys in. Identical vehicles; same journey, same time ... Phenomenally enough the girls' vehicle was through in moments, smiles and waves all round. The boys though? The nod took a little longer. Who'd have thought it!

One of the 'must haves' in the field is Tearfund tape, a thick roll of adhesive sticky tape that has more uses than an empty box of cornflakes and a pipe cleaner in the hands of a Blue Peter presenter! It is exceptionally versatile. I've seen it holding down tarpaulins, bundling timber together, holding on vehicle axle hubs, keeping the 'weather out' of the spilt sole of a walking boot ... The roads in Kosovo and Albania were in poor condition. It wasn't the narrowness or windiness that was a particular problem, but the potholes. Big slamming potholes, small juddering potholes, potholes you could see a mile off, others you couldn't see until you were in them. Teddington offer relief workers a well-thought out suggested kit list prior to assignment. I was hit in Kosovo with its one stark omission. I can see why some might feel embarrassed to offer suggestions regarding underwear; however, in my opinion, a range of scaffold-like maximum support bras are a bust-must. Out and about on the roads on one trip, I was painfully aware that I was inadequately dressed. Around the gear stick was the tape. What's a girl to do? Squirm in discomfort? With as much privacy as a multi-windowed vehicle could offer, I set to. The difference was phenomenal. With a few wraps here, a couple of straps there, I continued the journey delighted and at ease.

20/03/00

Had an excellent weekend in Prizren, doing a spot of getting away from it all with Paul V and Sa. The three of us had a great time, really easy people to live with for a weekend in an apartment with no power and a bathroom door that doesn't shut! We enjoyed the hospitality of a Prizren restaurant by night and sat sharing 'When I .....' stories. Had a fantastic brekky then into town. Sa and I strolled with purpose up towards an old fort overlooking the town, then had an unplanned meeting with two rather officious German KFOR troops that involved us being effectively frog-marched/ushered back down the hill, and receiving a stern ticking off. The thing was, there was a gap in the razor wire, and in our eyes the sign did not explicitly say 'No Entry!'

A minor detail of why the German troops were being quite so spectacularly officious that escaped mention in my email home was the contents of Sa's pockets, or rather the lack of contents. We were required to carry ID on us at all times. I got in the habit, always had my passport, carried my Tearfund ID and my KFOR 'theatre access' pass, acknowledging that I was officially allowed to be operating within the military theatre that was Kosovo. We got stopped by these soldiers and I held out my choice of IDs like a fan of cards. Sa, meanwhile, fumbled through her jacket pockets. The guys, satisfied with my proof, turned their attention to Sa. She produced a tattered tissue, and some Lypsyl! We were despairingly waved away by the men in khaki.

★ ★ ★ ★

I was with the team down in Kukes over Easter weekend, and had been struggling to pray for a while. Sometimes, I just lose sight of God. I lose awareness of him, question whether the whole God, Scripture, Jesus 'thing' is true and I find myself going through periods of doubt about the reality of Christianity. It doesn't happen often, but when it does – it's a tricky thing to share. It seems to me that a lot of Christians never doubt. They are always convinced of the existence, the living reality, the everything of God.

I cannot prove, beyond the shadow of a doubt, absolutely and totally that a loving, sovereign, Creator God exists. I can prove more satisfactorily that my mum exists – I can call her on the phone, touch her, I have photos – evidence that to my mind is absolutely conclusive. The trouble with Christianity is that no matter how many pointers I have, how many past experiences of God I can recall, how credible the Bible is and the teachings of Jesus are, how well the story of the crucifixion and resurrection stand up under scrutiny – a degree of faith is still involved.

Every time my faith lessens and my doubt increases I go through a similar pattern of backing off. Not easy to back off from an ever-present omnipotent God, but I give it a good go! My prayers will stop, I'll not read the Bible; various attractive temptations, I'll find all the more attractive. The trouble is – I don't have enough evidence to conclusively disprove the gospel. I'm stuck, can't prove it, can't disprove it! I tend to back off from God, doubting his existence while demanding a powerful demonstration of his presence – if he is indeed around!

Easter Sunday – one of the highs in the Christian calendar; I stood leaning on the balcony at the house in Kukes muddling in the middle somewhere of the 'I believe – I don't believe' continuum. Sa joined me on the balcony with a cup of tea.

'Sa, I can't pray at the minute.'

She suggested a walk to the lake.

We walked.

We sat beside the lake, in the shadow of the magnificent Mt Djalica. In that stillness, that peace, I shifted further up the continuum. Not beyond the edge of doubt, but to a place where it was taking more faith in 'nothing' to not believe, than it was taking faith in Jesus Christ to believe.

We prayed. Prayers poured out as we sat watching the clouds drift and the reflections on the water shimmer.

I'd love to say I had a blinding epiphany, a thunderbolt of revelation, stark writing on the wall – but I didn't. It was in the quiet that I met up with God once again. It wasn't in a powerful rock-shattering wind, an earthquake or a fire, but sitting still in the gentle whisper of the breeze, I became aware of God once again.

* * * *

I can vividly recall sitting and typing the following letter. The familiar view of the mountains out of my window offered little solace. It wasn't an outcome any of us had expected to the trials. A Dire Straits album was playing in my laptop, and as Paul walked quietly into my room, *Brothers in Arms* started. We didn't speak to each other, but for the length of the song he stood behind me in my chair. He put his hands on my shoulders and I held his hands there. The comfort of his touch released some of the well of emotion inside me, and tears rolled down my cheeks.

23/05/00

Dear All,

Yesterday the trial verdicts of 144 of the 1500 'missing men' of Gjakove were passed. For just over 12 months these men have been held as prisoners in Serbia. Many of them were snatched from their homes whilst playing no active role in the conflict of last year. Their 'crime' – 'acts of terrorism'. Two of the 'men' are 16 years old and have never held a weapon. The judge and jury allegedly consisted of Kosovo Serbs now living in Serbia. Each of the 144 has been given a sentence of 7-20 years. Appeals against the verdicts are unlikely to succeed.

To humanise these figures a little, this is how Tearfund Gjakove staff will have been affected. These are relatives and loved ones of the men and women who the team have lived amongst, worked with and loved for ten months. A former employee of Tearfund in Kukes has heard that her boyfriend has been sentenced. My right hand man who is 28 will not see his best friend until they are both 40. One of our engineers will not see his nephew until 2010.

The atmosphere here is stunned. Amongst a people who have lost so much, months after the peace treaty has been signed, greater losses are being felt. Candles of hope have been snuffed out. 'The reason for living disappeared yesterday' said one of our construction co-ordinators.

We in Gjakove need your prayers, as a city, as an organisation, as a team, and as individuals coming to terms with this news. Please pray for the men, their families and friends in Gjakove, for justice, pray as you can. Where petitions and protests and international pressure fail, we are reminded that thankfully, that is not all we have.

'For our struggle is not against flesh and blood, but against the rulers, against the authorities, against the powers of this dark world and against the spiritual forces of evil in the heavenly realms' (Eph. 6:12).

Thank you, Ems

The impact on the team was huge. This was an issue we had prayed about, talked about and had optimistically awaited the outcome of. The actual outcome could not have been all that much further from what we had hoped for.

★ ★ ★ ★

R&R's have the uncanny knack of arriving just at the right time. Or maybe, we are just able to keep going until the break, whenever it is scheduled for. I am at my most relaxed and effective when I know when my next break is. It makes a massive difference to me to be able to pace myself for a known duration of work. That said, there never seems a right time to put my work down, but undoubtedly I need to.

I took my break in Macedonia, once again with Dave and Sa. By that time, the three of us knew each other incredibly well – and still wanted to spend time with each other! Tiredness was at an unprecedented peak, and for those few days, we only walked from our lakeside apartment to the restaurant and the lake. The three of us managed to develop pretty slick routines to minimise energy expenditure: no alarm clocks would be set, consciousness would wander in or the first up would 'accidentally' wake the others, a bit of Bible study, a touch of prayer, before books, sun cream, cozzy, Frisbee, water bottles, volleyball, cameras, etc were all loaded into sarongs and towels and taken downstairs onto the grass beside the lake. A liquid rota evolved ensuring that the water or wine jug would not run dry.

★ ★ ★ ★

We used to hold praise and worship services together every six weeks or so. I loved those services. Someone would lead prayers, someone else worship, someone would preach, someone else lead a time of reflection (no notices or collection) – that was us being church. It's not easy to coast along in a congregation of ten people – you've got to be involved.

Though unorthodox, these services were cracking times. In one service three people had separately been asked to speak about aspects of the humanity of Jesus at difficult times, with reference to any biblical text from anywhere in Scripture, fairly loose boundaries. Stephen – Jesus being tired, Sa – Jesus being tempted, Gill – Jesus mocked: that was the only information these guys had been given. One of them was in

Kukes, one in Prizren, one Gjakove. They didn't speak with each other. Yet each of them spoke for the agreed minutes from the same passage. There are stacks of references in different gospels to Jesus being tempted, being mocked, times of tiredness – yet independently Stephen, Sa and Gill had chosen Jesus' prayer in Gethsemane.

The last service before the programme closed was colossal. We were once again beside the wide river Drin near Prizren. The venue was a sheltered, flattish grass area. It was a blue sky day and we set ourselves up at the foot of a steep incline, maybe ten metres from the water's edge.

For part of the service, a couple of us had made a cross with a piece of leftover timber from the distributions. For the sake of easy transport we hadn't attached the two pieces together. Dave and I arrived early at the Drin to set it up. It was spectacularly still that morning, the river coursed by silently, and the only company we had were the cattle wading in the shallows across the river. Dave was on the roof of the vehicle and quietly passed down to me the two pieces. They were massive. He dragged the upright over to the area we were meeting. The power of seeing a man hauling and struggling with this piece of timber symbolic of a cross was awesome. Watching him, I was really chilled. I don't think I have ever had so clear a picture of how it might have been for Simon the Cyrene to carry the cross to Golgotha.

By the time we had both pieces over where we wanted them, the rest of the team arrived. It was decided that it would be inappropriate to erect the cross as it might offend Orthodox believers living nearby. Instead we dug in and secured the upright only, and left the horizontal bar on the ground. We knew that this would be our last time of fellowship altogether. No one was in any rush. We worshipped, we prayed, we took communion, we wandered off and reflected on our time in the Balkans, and that's where the cross came in. People were given pieces of cardboard and asked to write down prayers – for Kosovo, for Albania, for colleagues, for people we'd worked with, for the region, for themselves, for whatever was on their hearts; whatever they would soon be leaving behind. When we'd done this, one by one we nailed them to the cross. It's a massive wrench just to jump out of a world you have been part of for so long. So many things are left undone, so many prayers left unanswered. As we drove back over the bridge towards Prizren that afternoon, the cross stood covered in our prayers. It apparently stood there for weeks.

Close down

By the time summer came, the view out of the back of the house had changed. Nearly all of the black, charred timber roof frames had been replaced, the majority of unfilled rectangular gaps now had windows or doors, and several of the damaged façades had been rendered over. Quite a turn around.

Part of my job was to co-ordinate the packing up, shifting out, and storage of kit, before handing it over to a team in Macedonia for servicing, reconditioning and onward deployment to other programmes. We had stacks of it – radios, computers, printers, telephones, vehicles, generators, batteries ... The team was shattered. I was shattered. Stress levels were high, we were all exceptionally task-focused yet aware that we wanted to pour some quality time into our colleagues and friends that we were about to leave. The result? Candles burning at both ends and in the middle!

My time and stress management at that time was non-existent. I'd fall asleep at my desk, in bed going through the five plus page inventory sheets with coloured markers, in the vehicles, anywhere. Everything got done in time, and having said round after round of goodbyes in Gjakove and then Prizren, our convoy of six vehicles headed to the Macedonian border. We were booked to fly out on Monday but rather than chance the changeable customs officers over the weekend, we left Kosovo on Friday.

As we rolled out of Kosovo, I sat beside Bekim as he drove. 'It's not really the job I'll miss.' He paused. 'Or the money. Or even the work. Tearfund is like family. It's like being with friends all day, every day. I'll miss that.'

Having got through the border with unpredictable ease, we met before heading down to Lake Ohrid for a couple of days before our flight. I still had to hand over all things logistical to a guy who'd been given the unenviable job of getting vehicles serviced, checking kit worked and preparing equipment for redeployment. This hand over was my last responsibility. I felt as high as a kite once I'd done it – a mixture of relief, satisfaction, excitement, and absolute exhaustion.

The rest of the team had gone on down to Ohrid ahead of Sa and I. As we set off on the three hour journey, I resolved to stay awake and keep Sa company as she drove. I held this commitment for about half an hour – then slept. The route was a difficult drive over mountainous terrain, in the dark. I was oblivious. Oblivious too to our eventual arrival in Ohrid later that night; to being picked up out of the vehicle, carried up two flights of the hotel stairs to my room, gently placed upon a bed, washed, the covers being pulled over me, and the lights going out. The next two days, I caught up on much of the sleep I'd missed over the previous few nights. On Sunday afternoon, we all drove back up to Skopje, hotelled overnight and flew the next day. Rach, Sa and I, in preparation for UK re-entry sat, feet on seats, painting our nails. Looking good – it's important!

Chapter 7

Back to the Bush

October 2000

Having bought a place with Sa, I headed back to Sudan. Part of me was scared by the prospect of going back to Malualkon, the place that I related with triggering off my epilepsy. However, I was also pleased to return to a place and a people I had so missed since I'd left. There was an element of pride involved, to prove I could take on this new role with epilepsy. On the DRT application form, you are asked what your biggest strengths and weaknesses are. The responses from various friends were overwhelmingly consistent. Strengths consistently included 'determination' – while weaknesses had 'stubbornness'! Determination is an asset, stubbornness a flaw – yet they have the same root. Whether my desire to get back to Malualkon was motivated more by my stubbornness or my determination is arguable.

This time, I had a new role as field co-ordinator, leading the Tearfund project team. Time does not stand still anywhere, not even southern Sudan. The local team had increased, the expatriate team had changed, new local officials were in post, the village market had moved, there were more water pumps around, the fruit tree saplings John had planted in the compound were growing, we had a thatched office, a therapeutic feeding centre (TFC), a very tidy 'team mess', an extra shower cubicle – with tapped water flow – no more bucket tipping! – the community meeting room had been finished. Not rocket science admittedly – but changes. In other ways though, nothing had changed. The war continued, people were displaced, malnutrition continued,

Tearfund were still trying to meet the needs of the people of Aweil East.

I was replacing Roz and the two of us had a superb catch-up time during the hand over. One of the qualities I admire most in Roz is her compassion. For the people of Sudan, that compassion runs deep; their lives, their plight, their situation has become an integral part of her being. She hasn't worked at being compassionate – she just is. Like Lord – like disciple!

My feelings the night before Roz took off were split. I felt ready to go for it with the project. That was tempered, though, by the fact that this would mean Roz was about to go, leaving me with the responsibility for the welfare of the team and the effectiveness of the project. It looked a bit serious. We prayed that last evening, one of those rambling prayers that roll on until that God-given peaceful fatigue stills tongues and quietens minds.

The next morning, the flight came. Hard goodbyes were said. My memory slipped back to the same scene of Rob leaving, twenty months ago. However positive I have felt about being in Sudan, always, as I've stood on the runway watching friends and colleagues take off, I have felt an incredibly powerful surging wave of isolation sweep over me. It's not that I wanted them to stay, nor that I wanted to go. It is a feeling that would make me resolve to 'get on with it'. Southern Sudan is one of the furthest points on the planet in many ways from the world I am familiar with, and though I always felt at home there, I knew I never was.

I stood silently watching the plane shrink. On the way back to the compound I felt a hand on mine; Daruka, an elderly lady of immense stature who swept our compound daily. She didn't say anything. Just caught and held my eye, nodded gently, and squeezed my hand. She knew.

3/11/00

'Cheeobak!'

I was cycling down the airstrip, in a manner prompting the *Chariots of Fire* soundtrack to come flooding to my mind. The sun was spectacularly set-ting away to my left. To my right, goats were licking more of themselves than I feel necessary to describe. Horned cows scattered in front of me as I pedalled. Behind me, the saddle was a little too pressing. I believe all that separated my rear portion from a severe looking metallic skewer were my knickers, and charity shop shorts.

Towards me cycled a stranger. We'd almost passed when I noticed a couple of extra features to his bike that I haven't seen in the Raleigh catalogues. Firstly, the Kalashnikov slung nonchalantly and snugly along the length of his crossbar. My eyes were then drawn to a metallic glint, and there it was, a sword whose blade overhangs both ends of the handlebars. It looked like something straight out of Captain Hook. Amazing how accessories differ the world over. I guess that's one of the stark ways that priorities differ at war and peace.

Sunday 5th Nov

Ben is preaching on Moses. Time and time again over the last few years I have been challenged, encouraged, amazed and inspired by the stories of this man of God. I think the bit that gets me most is Moses trying to squirm repeatedly out of God's claim that he is the one to deliver the Israelites. He comes up with many 'valid' reasons along the lines of 'I can't do it, use someone else', then after the miraculous exodus out of Egypt, bursts into a song of praise to God. The same God he was arguing with not so long before.

I've been 'Bozz' (as Tito, the local compound manager calls me) for a week – imagine. It's been good. I heard on Friday from the Programme Director that there has been no news with regard to funding. As things stand, we will run dry at the end of December. Shared this with the team on Friday and was surprised by the depth of my emotion as I spoke. Over the last 2 days, every quiet moment has been filled by images of me breaking it to the local staff, the authority, the community, etc. I feel an overwhelming sorrow about the prospect. We know full well that 2001 is going to be comparable to the suffering of '98, and yet we hang at the mercy of donors' purses. It is not the right time to leave.

Relief programmes are not cheap, especially in Sudan where the logistics of air freighting everything pushes up the price. Project resources – the unimix, seeds, tools, vehicles, the compound, salaries, all add up. Tearfund are in a fantastic position with the incredible number of supporters they have in the UK, generously tithing, responding to appeals and regularly putting their money in envelopes. The majority of NGOs are not blessed with such a solid financial base. Other funding – big money – comes from institutional donors, governments, structures such as the Disasters Emergency Committee and European Union. Needs assessments and viability studies are carried out, concept papers and project proposals written, budgets drawn up, objectives stated, negotiations ... negotiated, and so on. Then the wait.

Success – funding obtained.

Failure – funding denied.

Tweak it and come back – patience testing adaptations and discussions.

Six month projects start and are completed quickly. Funding for the next potential phase of work needs to be sorted as soon as possible, but delays occur, decisions are withheld, situations on the ground change, donor priorities shift.

The stress I felt with the potential closure was unnecessary. Funding was secured, the project continued. However, on the 5th November 2000 my foresight was not as confident and assured as my hindsight can be now.

Once again, I didn't know how or what to pray. I swung between the 'we need the money because we need to be here, Lord', and the 'if we don't get the money and we have to close down, that's fine, if that's your will, God' prayers. If I boldly prayed for funding and we didn't get it – God would have either not heard me, left my prayer unanswered or let me down. If I prayed the 'Your will be done' prayer – I'd never know if the prayer had been answered, or whether my praying it would have made the slightest bit of difference anyway. It always strikes me as odd to say to the omnipotent Lord of the Universe 'go for it, as you like, you choose what happens' – as if he's not going   to anyway!

* * * *

Monday 6th Nov
'Please implement the above…'

The 'above' was a memo from Teddington, that reduced me to a feeling of
absolute aloneness, wandering around the compound feeling confused,
tears teetering. The memo requested each of the field teams to hold an act
of remembrance on Sunday 12th November for Nick and Kevin.

I don't know exactly what the tears were for. Perhaps for Nick and
Kevin's' families and their loss, maybe for us as I remember back so vividly to this time last year, maybe some fear of the same thing happening as
I am flying 4 times over the next few days. I didn't want anyone to talk
to me, I just wanted somebody here who understood, who understands
that 'implementing the above…' is going to be hard.

Throughout the day thoughts drifted to Sa in Burundi, Dave in Bristol,
Sam in Kos, Gill near Wigan, Paul in Sierra Leone, Stan, Ben and the others. I wondered how they were feeling, I wanted to be with them, to have
somebody to hold me and say 'I understand Ems'. The feeling faded as
my thoughts turned to prayers, I hadn't realised the depth of emotion I
still feel about the guys' deaths.

I had a radio call when I got in from my afternoon – it was Rach. I never
realise how much I miss British banter until I get some. So 30 minutes
later on the HF we had naturally digressed to a small amount of social
chit chat, what are you doing for Christmas? When's your R&R?
Wrapping up conversation, I dropped it in:
'Romeo Sierra, I don't know if you're aware what anniversary this weekend is, over'
'….oh, good copy, I hadn't realised it had come round so quick, how are
you doing mate, over?'
That was enough, that was all I needed. Rach joined the Balkans in
spring 2000, but even though she wasn't there this time last year, I had
some sort of link with it all.

'Feeling lonely with it, and flying at the weekend, over.'
'Oh. Sorry. Mate I don't really know what to say, over.'
'You don't need to. I just needed someone to know, that's all, over.'

Looking forward to Loki on Thursday, it will be good to meet Anne, the
voice on the line.

Loki radio chats were a saving grace. I didn't meet Anne until a month
or so after I'd arrived in MK. She was one of the two Loki logisticians
and part of her responsibility was the twice daily security check with
each of the project sites. Anne was the only person outside of Mike Kilo
that I would speak to on a regular basis. Those chats were a tonic.
Business would be dealt with first, then on with the real matter of AOB.
Although lines were open and therefore what could be discussed was
limited, I am still amazed by the conversation we spanned. Anne had the
ability to hear and understand as much from words unsaid as words
spoken. It made a massive difference to my morale to have access to
someone on the 'outside' who I knew was bothered what was going on
and how I was, understood the situations we were facing, and whom I
trusted. I spent only a few days actually in Anne's company, but she probably knows better than anyone how that time in that place was for me.

Friday 10th Nov
Still in MK, flight in 2 hours. Something went wrong with the booking
so yesterday's plane was cancelled. If I get to Loki on time I have 10 minutes to get my connection to NBO[1] – Challenge Aneka never cut it this
fine. MSF[2] appeared yesterday saying that they have 9 severely malnourished children in their wards, can we take them. That brings us to about
16 known children in need of the therapeutic feeding centre (TFC). I
can't remember whether policy states that it's 20 or 30 to warrant
opening it, but numbers are definitely on the up. Seeking guidance this
weekend, particularly as funding is still unknown.

---

[1] Nairobi
[2] Médecins Sans Frontières

In recent months the project had been operating as an SFP – supplementary feeding project. A dry ration of unimix was distributed to children under five on a weekly basis to 'supplement' their other food sources. As nutritional situations worsened and more severely malnourished people presented, further action was necessary. That was where the TFC came into action. The TFC provided an initial intensive care phase where related medical complications were addressed and nutritional treatment started, of eight to ten meals per twenty-four hours. Following health improvement within seven days or less, a child would be transferred onto a further phase of intensive feeding four to six times a day. The centre was residential for the child being treated and also the dominant carer, usually the mother.

'Severely malnourished' was the standardised bench mark criteria for admission to the TFC. There were various ways of measuring this, including weight for height. At a stated height, globalised estimations of anticipated weight have been calculated. The bands or categories are: median, <85%, <80%, <70%, <60%. <70% classifies as 'severely malnourished' – these children are poorly. There are a number of other medical presenting criteria; and even to me, the children are not hard to identify; often severely dehydrated due to diarrhoea, vomiting, loss of appetite, extreme fatigue, and an incredible listlessness. While the west is fighting a seemingly losing battle with diseases linked with over consumption, in MK 'under consumption' continues to claim lives. There is no equity in the distribution of resources. I wonder whether the multimillions spent each year on diet and related issues come anywhere near the sum spent on the weight gain needs of parts of the developing world.

I found it easy, at times too easy, when I was back in the compound, to eat well. What I saw of the food shortages around me did not affect my diet. Rationalising that 'I need to eat in order to do my job, and make any kind of difference here', came quickly. I did struggle, however, with the ease with which I got to that viewpoint. Anyone surrounded by suffering of any sort needs to find ways of coping with it. I only allowed my emotions to be aired in Sudan at controlled times in controlled ways, after an incident, in fear that if I did give my emotions free rein they would make me ineffective. Since coming home, a lot of my fear, anger, confusion, sorrow and guilt have been exposed. Whilst I was there, I soaked up the stories, but unless those memories are talked and prayed out, they remain unaddressed.

Wed 15th Nov

13 severely malnourished under 5's have been identified, do we open the TFC? Yes we do. There's only 4 of us on the ground. Penninah's trying to evaluate her CHE (health ed), Alice needs to do a nutrition survey, Ben will carry most of the weight of the TFC – and me, fill in the gaps. Need a confirming nod from Fergus (Programme Director) and then all guns blazing, aim to be admitting on Monday morning. It is going to be manic. We have three days to get it shipshape for approx. 15 children and their mums. Have requested more personnel in the form of a nurse. Three expats is a little optimistic for running TFC and six supplementary feeding centres. I feel nervously excited at the thought. Need to make sure I'm disciplined R&R wise – it's going to be easy to get swept up in business and stay up here for too long, remind me of that if I haven't told you I'm off within a week – thanks!

★ ★ ★ ★

I slept outside in Sudan. An awesome privilege, that has now resulted in the habit of having my bedroom window flung open regardless of the temperature, except the Balkans winter. The sky in Africa always seemed unexplainably huge, the night time sky is no different. It remained a wonder. There was not a single night during my time in MK that anything obscured my view of the stars. I began to know the course and the timing of the path of the moon. I'm not surprised that when God had created the sun, moon and stars, he was chuffed when he 'saw that it was good' (Gen. 1:18). It still is.

The only minor negative of sleeping alfresco was the increased potential 'bug' problem. I did have a mozzy net around my bed, but that's not thick, is it? We're not talking substantial armour, we're talking something more akin to a net curtain. That was my sole protection against the fauna of Sudan. MK is riddled with scorpions, and they carry the disconcerting folklore principle that they always move in twos.

If you see one without a second, you try and sleep knowing that number two is somewhere nearby. My narrowest brush with scorpions caught me in the undignified position of being lingerie clad only. I was changing out of my skirt, picked up my shorts, gave them a brisk flick to shake out any creases – only to watch two resting scorpions tumble to the floor either side of my feet and scuttle off.

On another occasion I saw a scorpion scuttling towards the cook's foot as she sat. I shouted in Dinka what I thought was 'scorpion, scorpion!' The lady looked very confused and embarrassed by my outburst, and began swooshing her hands through her skirt, and trying to look behind her. Meanwhile, the scorpion had cleared off. I'd shouted 'Poo! Poo!'

Thursday 16th Nov

Have had a manic one – I've been back on the ground for nearly 48 hours and have not managed to get through a meal of any description without being interrupted by the radio, visitors, a meeting, etc. If this continues I will have to get Ben to set me up with a mobile intravenous line. 3 days until the TFC opens – confirmed at least 12 patients expected on Monday. This effectively means that we'll be in MK over Christmas. The excitement switches to nerves every now and then, followed by the giggles, the sort you get when you've no idea how to 'do it', but you know you have to, marvellous, love it!

Everyone out jogging this morning, thinking of starting a running club, is four enough?

... and ... relax

I had quite a bit of time but not a lot of laid on leisure. Growing up, I'd never been too aware of my stress. Sure, A levels took me a little closer to it than I liked, and University assignments often involved nail biting conclusions as deadlines approached, but until DRT, I'd never really had to consider how to be proactive in managing my stress. So many of my coping strategies are subconscious, I'd probably have felt like dialling a friend's number and having a good jaw. I quickly realised my existing strategies had a limited effectiveness in Sudan. I had to find some new ones.

I started to pray more, partly because of the extremity of the situation. I start speaking to God, wanting and expecting to hear from him when my perceived need of him was high i.e. in the middle of a war zone. With shameful consistency, the quality, discipline and honesty of my prayer life plummets every time I come home, as though I need God less in the UK. Partly though, God became more of a close friend as I was apart from my human buddies.

I wrote, as I did in Sudan first time round. On an almost daily basis something of the day's events, thoughts, feelings would make it to the laptop, and ultimately down internet lines, into 'Stratt's log'. Quite possibly the act alone of writing, without knowing that people were reading it, would have served a valuable purpose.

Running; even though the environment was physically demanding in terms mainly of the heat, my working hours were sedentary. Don't exercise and apathetic physical lethargy develops. Exercise and feel invigorated. I was less emphatic on that theory on those first few 6 am mornings as my reluctant body struggled to keep up with my more enthusiastic mind along the routes round the village.

Reading – absolutely anything. *The Count of Monte Cristo, What's So Amazing About Grace?, Cosmopolitan, Just Like Jesus, Round Ireland with a Fridge, Breakthrough French – Study Pack 2, Captain Corelli's Mandolin* (again), I'd read it all. The girl whose previously most illustrious reading phase involved the Blackberry Farm books had developed the capacity to consume a book a week. I had an incredible ability to lose myself in the pages.

My levels of personal discipline with all these hobbies reached unexpectedly dizzy heights. Ordinarily, I can be quite effective in squeezing out prayer time, talking myself out of a run. In Sudan – I got into a routine. Five mornings a week I'd run. I'd pray after my morning shower before radio check. I'd write after my evening shower before dinner time. I think this was the assignment where I got to grips with the responsibility of looking after myself properly; nearly always eight hours sleep, doing what I could to not miss meals and stopping work at a decent time. The pocket size embroidery kit 'Poppies in a Pot' once again remained unopened – I couldn't do everything!

Friday 17th Nov

6:00 running
7:30 led devotions Daniel 3
8:00 brekky
8:30 meeting with counterpart about closing a feeding centre
9:30 terminated a member of staff's contract who had been with us for 19 months
10:00 rechecked his severance pay – 4 months worth of salary!
10:30 paperwork – generating stuff for filing
12:30 contemplated filing – didn't activate
13:00 lunch
13:15 guitar – 1st time in 4 weeks, wondered why I'm not yet accomplished
14:00 TFC visit – looking good
14:30 time with team, not really sure what else, but I was busy doing whatever it was
17:00 weekly report
18:00 finish.

Spent big chunks of today on the radio – not a complaint, like it. Also spent quite some time running out the office to watch Antonov (bombing) planes – four today, increasing in number. I never thought plane spotting would be something I'd get into, amazing how interesting planes overhead can become when you know they are of the potential bomb dropping genre rather than holiday maker sort. Said goodbye to Fergus, he has promised face packs from the UK – fantastic, good boss!

Time with team – bomb pit practice

Leading devotions – pre-Tearfund, this was an alien concept to me. I hadn't done it. Actually, to be fair, praying out loud in a small group setting was still a novel and daunting concept. As for leading devotions, putting together 15-20 minutes worth of prayer, sung worship, scriptural sharing and discussion didn't come easy. In a small team, you get to know each other pretty well. You don't have the liberty of walking away from each other at 17:00 each night. At home you see your Pastor once, maybe twice a week. House group? Every couple of weeks. In team? – 24/7. Any kind of behavioural masks cannot weather that level of exposure. If you threw a strop, had a lazy moment, or made a bitchy comment, chances are someone in your team noticed. You couldn't hide.

It does make for a lot of reality relationship-wise. I think I said more prayers of confession in Sudan than anywhere else. It's hard to lead a talk on forgiveness when you are holding onto a gripe over one of your teammates! It's tricky to sing that 'God is good all the time', when the health educator has just spent her afternoon grieving with the family of a child who was burnt to death in an attack on their village. It is testing to thank God for his bountiful provision when you know one of the nurses is disheartened about the lack of improvement in the condition of the fifteen malnourished children in the TFC.

Appraisals are always an interesting time relationally in 'Team'. It seems to be human nature that if ninety-nine positive comments are listed, the one insignificant 'area for development' is that which burrows into appraisees' souls. However gracious and mature we are, appraisals in a 24/7 team test the strongest of relationships, let alone any on thinner ice! I've come to the conclusion that they are less of a science than an art.

The lunar menstrual cycle is pitifully inconsequential in terms of effects on moods in comparison with the R&R cycle:

- Week 1: 'Why on earth am I doing this?' Post R&R blues, climatic and situational readaptation
- Week 2: 'Great to see everyone – I could do this forever, and never need another break'
- Week 3: Routines once again have become habitual, contented and functional
- Week 4: Still contented and functional,
- Week 5: Fatigue raises its head, yawns replace laughs, glares replace grins
- Week 6: Countdown begins, Demob delirium, 'I don't care', 'the whole world is wonderful'
- ....and relax............

I'd avoid appraisals in weeks one and five. Week six, people agree and sign anything. Weeks two, three and four – that's the slim window of opportunity. Trouble is, the team members are all at different stages of the cycle, and tend to be on R&R one or maybe two at a time, depending on the size of the team. You have to do them all at once, to get the jolly 'building, developing and affirming' thing over and done with, avoid the paranoia of one team member feeling 'targeted' (this is enhanced with the reaction some team members experience due to their malarial prophylaxis!)

Despite these tribulations, I do love appraisals – getting and giving them. If the difficulties can be overcome, they are a real boost.

Sunday 19th Nov

Roz used to make pizza in the diesel drum oven – naturally the team expect the same culinary wizardry from me. Feeling confident I took to the task. I never smelt copious amounts of smoke on Roz, nor saw her face covered in ash, nor did I see her limp from kicking the 'door' closed rather too aggressively with sandals on. However, I was able to share 'one I prepared earlier'. Main lesson less than 1 can of tomato paste concentrate is probably sufficient.

There's rumours of a cow/goat disease in the area, sounding similar to foot and mouth. I do acknowledge the potential nightmare of this for the community, but on a selfish level, I am not strongly opposed to the ban we as a team have imposed on goat consumption. Nyama choma (roast goat) is not on my favourite meal list, not least because of the suspicious feeling that you have eaten not just meat but a generous wad of the goat's hair because of the carpet presence in your mouth. The fact we're on tuna today is just fine!

★ ★ ★ ★

Imagine the sights, the home side underdogs, the away team top guns, the chants, the stamping, the speeches and opening ceremony, the local dignitaries ensconced in the hospitality area. Add to it a few anomalies from the weekly scenes of Match of the Day – volleyball not footy, barefoot not £100 trainers, airstrip not stadium, sandy dirt not turf, overt armoury not subtle head sets for security of the big guys. There we were yesterday afternoon, soaking up the atmosphere, chanting out our allegiance to Mike Kilo in the baking sun. It was fantastic, crowds were well in the hundreds.

MK took the first 2 games, so assumed we'd won. So.....we started a 'friendly' to release some of the tension and diffuse the humiliation of the commissioner's dream team. We lost, then the opposition claimed it wasn't a friendly and that they'd won on aggregate. When it comes to sport and our team have won already, I can't sit too comfortably and hear the opposition shouting of their victory. What followed was probably one of my most frightening times in Sudan – all over a volleyball match!

It got dark. Then, it transpired that one of the guys from another NGO had 'promised' about 40 people lifts home. Fine, nothing to do with us. But he had a puncture – so the big wigs were stranded. We have a very clear rule that we do not leave the compound after dark. However, it is not done to leave these guys in the dark. So I was swamped within a huge adrenaline pumped crowd touting their case as to why Tearfund should take them home. The rest of our team were back in the compound and, in spite of having a handset, I found myself feeling vulnerable. I was offered an armed guard to do the journey (we have another rule, no weapons in the vehicles!), then watched in dismay as various gun-toting guards tried to conceal their weapons from my eyes. After a few minutes of saying 'no' with much conviction whilst trying to appease the disappointed (and important!) Commissioner, the 'lift promiser' had repaired his puncture, 2 of my team came down, picked me up and we locked ourselves away in the compound.

I was hopping when I got back to the compound. It wasn't the prospect of driving in the dark that bothered me, nor the protracted arguments about our vehicles carrying weapons. What scared me was the crowd. It happened so quickly. One minute orderly cheering beside a volleyball court, the next I was surrounded, being jostled, pulled one way and then another by anonymous arms. I could see a few skirmishes on the fringes of the throng. I had rarely felt vulnerable in Mike Kilo. With the high emphasis on security, we knew our potential risks, and were as equipped as we could be to face them. Tell me of imminent potential bombing, and that's OK. Put me alone in the middle of a hyped-up sports crowd firing off celebratory shots – result: scared Em.

I'd missed the radio check by the time I got back to the compound. I tried to call Anne in Loki anyway. She wasn't there. I showered in the moonlight, and took myself off to bed, finding solace in Pachabel's

Canon. I was exhausted and relieved that the grass fence perimeter of the compound provided a barrier – psychological at least – from the outside world.

Chapter 8

See Amid the Winter's Dust

Merry Christmas and a Happy New Year

Thursday 14th Dec

Shona arrives tomorrow. I had cabin fever today. I have left the compound twice, for a total of 15 minutes, not good at these office days. Still, got a good start to next week planned – off to meet a farmer on Sunday, a Commander on Monday, perhaps a bit of SFP[1] on Tuesday – much better. Dismissed someone today, employed someone else – so a good balance there. Got very excited chatting with the UNICEF humanitarian principles guys about the possibility of a school for ex-child soldiers. Apparently I gave some water to the leader of the project about 22 months ago.

I have spent good quality time with the team, relationships have deepened lately, I think an Antonov or 2 sniffing around, and the occasional raid far to the west is uniting us slowly. Looking forward very much to Shona being here, have had rock solid recommendations from 3 trusted friends who have met her. I've missed having a buddy – great colleagues and team mates, no problem – but could use some quality friendship out here.

Saturday 16th Dec

Dropped off a family whose child was severely malnourished and had a chest infection. The father was emaciated and the mother had open TB. Although we could feed up the child, we can't admit them because of the

---

[1] SFP – Supplementary feeding programme

risk of infection from the mother. There is no clinic or resource for TB treatment in the area at all, so, mother and probably child are just going to have to wait for death. Amidst the ample resources and medical expertise in the team etc, somehow seems totally inadequate to let someone die. But, harsh realities and therefore decisions of this place. I took the family to Aquem, the MSF hospital, and they will assess her and make that call, not one our nurse felt comfortable doing.

I brought back 3 more children for the TFC in the vehicle. I had one of those times where the futility and lack of justice in this war just appals me. Sometimes out here, I switch to a mechanical autopilot, other times I feel a depth of emotion I can do nothing with but pray. The Commander struts around wearing Rayban sunglasses, with his immaculately kitted out élite armed guard of 6, whilst just metres away kids are washing themselves and drinking in the water that spills from the pump. Water that had hundreds of feet standing in it, downstream of where the cattle are drinking.

I was listening to a cassette, and the lyrics to the song or prayer playing were: *Can a nation be changed*? That's it; a petition to God. As this played in the vehicle, the tears brimmed in my eyes as my despair was replaced by a flicker of hope, enough to believe in, just a bit. We have our diplomats, we engage in peace talks, but ultimately, surely, peace can only come here through God. My prayer is that Sudan will be changed, will turn back to God.

The tape stopped, the vehicle kept rolling, the mothers in the back, one by one, threw up with travel sickness, one all over me: my thoughts changed but my prayer remains.

Sunday 17th Dec
Christmas Eve this time next week, imagine! The advent calendars are nearing completion, the turkey is on its way to Loki, staff time off is sorted, so far removed from a UK Christmas. 674 displaced people turned up in Aquem with no provisions. They live near the railway and

have had their homes burnt and looted, now are left with no blankets, shelter, food, water, etc. bit of a pickle. We're sitting here storing hundreds of UNICEF 'IDP' kits'[2] – but have no authority to release them without a UNICEF nod, something to start the week off with!

Tuesday 19th Dec

Our recent, mini nutrition assessment (Dec 10-12th) has shown that nutritional status is the best it has ever been since Tearfund arrived in MK. This is probably due to many things; there have been 2 years of feeding, food security, health education and health interventions; but also the community have just harvested. Our big dilemma at the moment as an organisation is should we continue to distribute at times like this, i.e. relative plenty (immediately post harvest), or will we contribute to potential dependence on relief support? There's a concept of 'do no harm', and I am not convinced that we are 'doing most good' by handing out now. Within 4-6 weeks when the harvest has been utilised and no more food is available, that's a different matter. I think at the minute that we would serve the community better if we concentrated on encouraging harvesting of indigenous fruits, roots, veg which are abundant at the moment; education on food storage practices, etc. In our TFC we have 9 children currently, having just discharged a big batch. All 9 are severely malnourished following bouts of illness (measles, fever, diarrhoea, etc) – NOT purely because there is not enough food to go round.

To feed or not to feed?

These are some of the topics I loved – the stretchers. There is a real danger in ongoing relief situations – like Sudan – for external support to go beyond providing immediate much-needed assistance, and systematically start to undermine local coping mechanisms. It's no new phenomenon during the hunger gap between harvests, when food does become scarce, for the southern Sudanese to rely on indigenous wild

---

[2] IDP – Internally Displaced People

plants and trees – eating not just the fruit, but in some cases leaves and roots. This isn't as a result necessarily of exceptional famine, or due to mass displacement, this is a way of life for people whose home is in a geographically hostile part of the world.

The issue of 'do no harm' has become quite a hot potato as agencies are increasingly called to account for their actions. Tearfund had been feeding in MK for two years, and our concern was that we were offering the same programme around the calendar. As the only agency doing feeding in the area, breaking the distribution schedule would have repercussions on many levels. In the end, we honed down further the number of children we wanted to specifically target over the coming weeks, increased the impetus of our health education work and developed complementary education sessions to highlight other food sources.

It's easy to become governed by habit and the 'way we've always done things', and lose sight of the current situation on the ground. There'll probably be enough malnourished people in southern Sudan to justify continuing feeding programmes for several years and it is our responsibility to be flexible within what we do, moulding it and shaping it to meet the needs on the ground, as and when they vary.

Thursday 21st Dec

I'm listening to a cassette of Kates reading 'Where is my bone?', Bex being the 'beep beep' horn during the wheels on the bus, Sara salvaging the microphone from being consumed by both girls, Mummy justifying that she is eating just 3 scones for breakfast as opposed to the popular opinion of 8 and Daddy, well obvious in his absence so far. All very refreshingly normal and familiar after a tricky day.

Hard day – just after lunch one of our child to child educators, Ben, asked to speak to me. Ben is early twenties and became a delighted father for the first time a few weeks ago. With dry but red eyes looking straight into mine, he stood tall and informed me that his 'sister had been brought to the health clinic this morning, but now is passed away.

Would it be at all possible to ask for lifting to Pariak, sorry for intrusion.'

Minutes earlier, as a fun-loving youth worker he had collected the football to take out and play with the children. Now, as the oldest man present of his family, he was bearing the grief of losing his sister with stoical dignity. In his young eyes incomprehension at the loss, on his shoulders the acceptance that this is the way of life that he knows so well.

We prayed as a team for the family, for comfort, for peace in shattered hearts. I prayed in faith, not questioning why, just accepting this grief that we had been invited to glimpse. I drove the vehicle to the clinic with Shona, greeted the girl's mother and other relatives and we lifted the covered body onto the bed of the pick-up. The drive is only 8km, it seemed to take an age. I drove slowly in reverence and respect for my vulnerable passengers. As usual the kids came tearing up yelling 'Kawaga' in excitement, waiting for a wave and a smile. I felt that they should know this was not a time for joy. We should have been in a hearse, but we were bouncing down an uneven track in a pick-up in silence. As we approached the home, women started wailing – having wordlessly been told of the reason for our visit. Children stood nervously at a distance in huddles, touching each others' arms, just looking on. Old men lowered their heads. Young men helped as we lifted the girl down onto a mat in the shade as sisters, friends, aunts and her mother gathered to weep and mourn openly. I drove away. A time for everything.

★ ★ ★ ★

Rach and Fiona have just called from northern Kenya, they've closed down for Christmas and are heading for Nairobi, festive spirit oozing down the radio. 'We're just having a party in the back of the pick-up'! Versatile vehicles. Really good to hear from them, they even sang We Wish you a Merry Christmas, quite a legitimate break of radio protocol considering the season! They've promised to hit the shops in Nairobi and send a suitable entry in the mail pouch for Christmas. In spite of the distance, I feel well cared for by friends and family this year. People have gone to big efforts to put things in the post – feel well loved.

Friday 22nd Dec

Cecilia – a beautiful baby. First born of Sammy, one of our SFP feeding assistants and Nyabol, a cook. Stark – the comparison of touching death yesterday and cradling life today. As I held her, I caught myself wondering where her life would take her. What would her Sudan be like? Would she see peace? A brand new life, fresh, clean, uncontaminated, innocent – so many places to go, so much to see, living in a mud hut whilst her country is at war around her. Potential. I was asked to pray for her, so I thanked God for her, and asked for his continued blessing on her life, meant it, all of it.

Saturday 23rd Dec

Am: I had an insect in my ear last night. Buzzing and tickling around – for a girl of sensitive ears, quite an ordeal. There I was in the darkness stretching my ear, shaking my head violently, having a good scratch and poke – but no joy, every time I lay down bzzzz, tickle bzzzz tickle. Lying on my side, being observed by one of our guards, I poured water from my bottle into my head. Minutes later, I guessed the drowning would be complete. I sat up, shook and listened. Silence. I slept.

Plane came yesterday, and with it a mail pouch – they don't normally have 'Handle with care' instructions, but then they don't normally have a bottle of wine in! Christmas naughtiness from our log in Loki, utilising the mail pouch service to its best by sending the team what they really want. It's been sitting on my desk tantalisingly within reach – a little gift that will not be opened ahead of time.

Pm: Just back from a needs assessment of some internally displaced people (IDPs) forced to flee their homes because of insecurity. 43 children allegedly burnt to death in raids and subsequent torching of homes and surrounding forest. Precious ceramic cooking pots deliberately trampled, metal ones taken to support the war efforts of the opposition. Water-carrying containers stolen or punctured. Food stores of treasured grain harvests smashed open, grain spilled out to the floor and home owners only able to look on as the raiders' horses are allowed to take their fill. I sat chatting (through a translator) with the chief – he'd recently lost his young son in the burning bush around the village during a raid. I asked him what his peoples' immediate priority needs were – as I gazed around us at temporary grass shelters whose diameter was less than my height that are housing 6-7 people – 'Food, cooking pots and water containers – we've come with nothing, this will be enough.' Not an unreasonable man.

I got back to the compound to hear from Anne that 16MT of unimix is likely to be dropped on the 7th, and other supplies in at the end of next week, fantastic news, we need it. Had a drink and some food and shared an animated and slightly 'adapted' Christmas story with our staff before offering their gifts of soap, oil and sugar, then cracked on with the weekly report. I need to get away – just for a while. I clearly remember George looking me in the eye 20 months ago saying with a weary smile 'Em, I just want to be 26 for a bit.' I want to be 26 for a bit. Time to stop being calm, in control and leave the demands. Time to soak my feet in a bucket of water, play some music, read some new e's and just stop.

Sunday 24th December
'Aren't those rats' footprints on the icing?'
My first words to the team this morning. Consensus – rats had run a merry dance across the lovingly baked choccy cake whilst we slept. Shona's face dropped, she put down her fork load of cake, Anthony started scraping off the icing, giggling, Damaris whooped and said 'imagine', I got a plate and helped myself to a generous (it is Christmas) portion of de-iced sponge. Shona's face blanched as I put fork to mouth and the team's laughter gradually subsided. 'I've got to toughen up', she said, contemplating another mouthful, but unable to turn the thought to action. It tasted fine, and there were no visible droppings – hygiene standards out here perhaps wouldn't gain me an A+ in Home Ec. classes, but they're real.

After breakfast, I slipped into a hammock. Spent the entire morning reading, could have taken root into the afternoon but we'd agreed to go fishing with another agency at the nearest river. The river is drying up, as it does in the dry season. It's muddy and a favourite watering hole of cattle. In I went up to my knees – that's when the questioning starts. 'Can you catch such and such disease in here?', 'Did you hear about the crocodiles at so and so?', 'Seems like a perfect breeding ground for deadly whatsit'. It never happens when everyone is on the side, people wait until the first one has dared to go in. I stood my ground undeterred for a few minutes then thought better and retreated to read on the bank.

I'm not good at staying out of water for long. There were a couple of boats, hollowed out tree trunks, so – boating time. It was going fine until a spectator decided I was going in the wrong direction. He issued instructions to a local child who leapt to my 'aid', grabbed the boat sharply and disturbed my precarious balance, introducing me unceremoniously to the waters below. Once you're wet, you're wet! Swimming time – it felt amazing. Not many Christmases go by when you get to play in rivers, in heat and freedom.

Like all good days out, sadly home time comes. In various degrees of dampness we clambered into the hard top. I foolishly overestimated the dryness of the mud, and underestimated the heaviness of our vehicle – combined errors equalling one Toyota, bull-bar deep in muddy clay. I tried reversing out – no joy, engaging 4WD – no joy. Spoke to Geoff in the other vehicle, we sorted out the tow line, passengers out, took the strain, 2nd gear, and away we were, sorted. To come out of 4WD I had to claw handfuls of claggy clay from the wheels, probably very good exfoliation for my palms, might bottle it and see if the Body Shop are interested.

Christmas Eve has come to an end, pleasantly weary from a good day of rest and play. It's certainly gone some way to address the unequal balance of excess work in the last few days. Cards are all up, balloons ready to blow, pressies wrapped ... Driving through the bush, waving greetings at friendly neighbours, singing at the top of my voice today, I felt another wave of how fortunate I am to be in this place at this time, doing this stuff.

Dec 25th
MERRY CHRISTMAS ALL, SINCERELY!

I'm sitting here with a 'revitalised face', 'refreshed feet', multi-coloured nails, tinsel round my neck, gum in my mouth and new knicks on – oh, I am wearing other stuff, they're just some of the new bits! It's Christmas day, we're just heading out for supper to the other agency's compound. I've had a good day, got God where he should be – start, middle and end – quality. Unfortunately one of the cooks didn't show this morning at no notice and so the roast dinner was adapted at short notice to fried turkey, rice, cabbage and carrot stir fry – not a sprout to be seen! Still hooters, crackers, paper hats, pressies all round adorned the mess as 'good scoff' was had by all.

Thursday 28th December
Bit of a nightmare yesterday, started after breakfast with the now infamous words 'PC[3] we have.....' you just know the next words are going to be '.....a problem'. I'm becoming a little more accustomed to this phrase, so didn't even break from my tooth brushing rhythm! To cut a painfully long story at least a little shorter, one of our local staff, James, got drunk on Christmas Day, and at night smashed a bloke over the head with a plank, knocking him unconscious, spilling much blood and rendering him concussed for 2 days, unable to turn his head or open his mouth. James was put in prison pending investigation. On Boxing Day, another member of staff, Akech, got drunk and at night (sounding familiar?) smashed a woman over the head, spilling much blood and leaving a gash about 2 inches deep in her skull. Akech is in prison pending investigation.

---

[3] Project Co-ordinator

These are 2 of our best loved and trusted guys. They have been in trouble before for similar offences. They may find themselves forcibly conscripted to the army as they will be unable to pay the fine this time. I've been trying today to prayerfully work out how we as an organisation should respond to this. Hard because if these 2 lose their jobs they have little chance of completing their education, and then, a life of little hope. My decision is to have suspended them from duty pending their court cases. I do not want to dismiss them pre trial and verdict, innocent until proven...., but at the same time I do not feel it is appropriate to have them working right now. Trying to do what is right and what is fair. If they are found guilty (which they pretty definitely will be) – I will have to dismiss them. I told them my decision this afternoon, one of my worst PC duties yet. They're due in court in about 2 weeks. Damaris and Anthony are gutted, they put so much time into the guys.

Whilst this was happening, one of our TFC children started to fit last night. He deteriorated today, and is hardly conscious. We've just arranged for him to be transferred to the hospital, again hard on Shona and Damaris – they're naturally really concerned about the prognosis.

So the team are a little emotionally battered. Work continues, and one real asset has been that the 4 of us have got a lot closer as a team as a result of these external pressures.

Friday 29th December
Good day – had a surprisingly productive time. I'm trying to minimise our 'weak links' within the project and work at increasing the quality and effectiveness of our work. Have been drawing up frameworks, asking questions that produce another 3 questions rather than any answers, and just getting down to some solid, stretching, thinking. Enjoyed it. Do I sound like a mission statement at the moment?

I've just finished my weekly catch up meeting with Shona, tea shop in the market last week, walk down the drop zone today. It's a little distracting to have to shake so many hands during a meeting without losing the focus of the conversation, but stacks better than sitting in a hot, sticky office. The food store is heaving once again, looks much better, I was beginning to get a little concerned as to what we could concoct with a multitude of cans of sweetcorn, tomato puree, coffee, peanut butter and not a lot else – there's a challenge for Ready, steady, cook!

Sunday 31st December

I've just called level 3 – that means our security has deteriorated to such a point that we are confined to the compound because of a possible threat, and are effectively in a 'preparing for potential evacuation' state (I'm now sounding like a security plan as opposed to a mission statement!). The SRRA[4] security man came by last night to advise us not to be overly concerned by the rumours we'd heard of the PDF[5]. We hadn't heard any rumours! Without giving that away, I continued to probe gently for info. The very fact he came means trouble. If we go level 3 and subsequently 4 (out) the SRRA have a lot to lose, agencies will not be keen to locate in insecure areas, programs will be limited, etc. so for them to report that 'it' is nothing, generally means they want us to remain always at level 2 (normal operations). I spoke with Geoff – acting PC of IRC[6], and we are agreed if we cannot move freely, then level 3 it is. The food trunk is packed (priorities), water jerry cans full, quick run kits restocked, fuel tanks full (my internal one and the vehicles) – so now, we relax!

Later – I am a caged animal! I have written emails, studied from my French pack, read, bathed my feet, listened to music, paced back and forth round the compound. As soon as I'm told I can't go out, all I want to do is go out – normally I'd crave a restful Sunday like this. Why is it that all my teenage rebellious urges are kicking in 10 years later than the norm?

---

[4] Sudanese Relief Rehabilitation Association
[5] People's Defence Force
[6] International Rescue Committee

Insecurity

For days over that period of time round New Year, I seemed to spend most of my waking hours focused on security. Other things like running a project played second fiddle to staying safe. It was the biggest difference from my first trip to Sudan. Then I had responsibil-ity just for myself and to follow the PC's call. Second time – it was my call to make. Man, did I pay more attention to the planes in the sky, the word on the street, the movements of the soldiers, information from Loki, develop-ing trust within the team and local staff and so on. That potential risk was always there. Priority number one – safety of the team. There was one occasion when we were categorically told via   several of our 'reli-able sources':

'Mike Kilo will be bombed tomorrow.'

This was difficult news to share with people. No casual way of slip-ping that one into dinner conversation.

The next day the team were moving around the compound as chil-dren do in musical chairs. Only the 'chairs' to dive on were the bomb pits. The music stopping was the Antonov!

We weren't bombed.

We were told with 'absolute confidence' it would happen the next day – it didn't. Some of the team risked moving a little further afield, others didn't.

'Definitely' the next day. No bombs. By day four, it was becoming a bit of a joke. The tension was easing. We didn't get sloppy, we were aware of where our nearest pit was, we carried our quick run bags with us, we listened for ominous engine drones in the sky; but we lost that crippling sense of the foreboding 'inevitable'. You adapt, you have to, or you are crippled by 'what might never happen'. It takes its toll though, and when you come out of that environment you realise how far removed your 'Sudanese normality' is from your 'home normal-ity'. For months after leaving Mike Kilo the sound of aeroplane engines would still lift my eyes to the sky. Fireworks or similar sounds would take a fleeting moment to 'OK' mentally – not gunfire. We re-adapt.

Monday 1st January

Happy New Year – we saw it in in memorable style. After an evening of indulging in seasonal excesses – that naturally I later regretted – of pineapple rings, and lasting until 9:10pm, I was out for the count. As the all-night worship pounded away in the church, I left 2000 to the history pages. At 12:15am the church woke me with considerable gusto and welcomed 2001 passionately. Had a really God-full time of devotions this morning, seeing out one year, and welcoming the next – quality time with the Lord.

Following various non-tallying accounts of the security situation, we have returned to level 2. I accompanied the SFP distribution and had a lovely day out, getting back a little later than usual. I love getting out the office and getting down to the real work that we're here to do.

Tuesday 2nd Jan

Yesterday afternoon the plot darkened regarding James and Akech. Akech's case will be sorted out of court, because the woman he hit was

The church at Mike Kilo

Photo: Sarah Casey

one of his uncles' wives. James, however, hit a highly trained elite soldier.
James had been taking sanctuary at the TFC, day and night, as threats had
been made by Deng (the man he hit) to take his life. When I say threats,
I mean an angry man walking round the village with a loaded gun, trying to shoot him. Having weighed up my responsibility to the team, staff,
beneficiaries, general public and also James and Akech, I asked them not
to return to Tearfund property prior to their cases being resolved. I
explained why, and they clearly saw that a crazed man seeking revenge
with a shotgun should not be encouraged in any way at a TFC full of
mums and children under 5. Rather than me just turf them out to play
cat and mouse with this man, I promised I would speak to the SRRA,
and try and arrange some protection for them.

I did this when I got back, and it all went incredibly grim. Deng had
been spoken to by the authorities earlier about not shooting James, and
was advised to wait for the court case. Deng was having none of it. The
SRRA wanted James out of MK ASAP – because he was not only at risk,
but also the community were in danger because of his presence if shooting did kick off. They were fully expecting these threatening words to be
turned into action. They asked me to ask James to hand himself over to
the police, where, though not free, he would be safe. I tried, James did
not want to go, he was not ready – we chatted amicably but I was getting nowhere so left it.

It got to the stage where Deng was in the market (2 minutes from us)
and the SRRA security, fearing a shooting incident, insisted James be
moved out of MK. Tearfund's was the only vehicle that could assist with
this. I agreed that if James was willing I would drive him the 15 minute
journey to the police station, expecting a pleasant easy trip with no problems. The call came from the SRRA on the handset that they were ready,
I drove to James' place and he bolted. Everyone was tense. Deng had not
been seen for a few minutes, no-one knew quite where he was. James was
caught and quickly bundled into the vehicle. The SRRA and security
jumped in surrounding him and I drove. I drove like I have not driven in
a long time to get out of this place, like the wind. I was very frightened.

Prior to all this, it seemed clear to me and the team that every effort should be made to get James to the safety of a cell. I was concerned that Deng could enter our compound here or the TFC, believing James to be inside and have a few random shots – we are talking about an innocent man who was cracked on the head and can't yet talk – one angry guy. At the police station, we got up to leave, and I went to James to shake his hand, just as we always do to say goodbye. He looked straight at me, glaring, refused my hand and walked past me. I was gutted. Fighting back hot tears, I got into the vehicle with the other guys to drive back home. I didn't want his thanks or appreciation; I was just trying to do what I felt I had to. I've been replaying all this again and again, trying to work out where I should have butted out, not compromised my own safety. It's one of those scenarios I haven't come across in a role play exercise in the comfort of a conference centre suite. Might propose it at the next course I'm on.

One of the biggest 48 hours of emotional drain I've gone through here. I tried to call Anne on the radio last night but she'd left the office. I tried Rob in Burundi – but the selcall wouldn't go through. I didn't want to talk about it, just to hear a comforting familiar voice, that's all.

James and Akech

In spite of the minor detail of being a nation at war, law and order amongst the civilian population is pretty tight in Sudan. I fear being a victim of petty crime in the UK far more than I did in Sudan. Standards are high and penalties are swift and severe for anyone who steps out of line. This was the first 'civil' act of violent crime I'd heard about since I arrived in Mike Kilo. I was surprised by it and by the fact it was James and Akech, who were two of our most senior, most responsible staff. I not only trusted them, I liked them as well. James had a kind of Rasta cap he'd wear day in, day out, and was so laid back he was practically horizontal. Akech had a tenacious sense of humour that could cut across cultural differences and a cheeky audacity. The extent of the injuries they inflicted was substantial. Deng's power of speech was still not right by the time we left Mike Kilo in March, and as for the lady – Akech's aunt – her head took months to heal.

There was a lot of pressure to get the decision of how to deal with the situation 'right'. Everyone was waiting for my call. The police authorities had even stalled their action, waiting first to see what Tearfund's response would be. How do you extend 'Christ-like' forgiving grace whilst recognising that there is a need for justice and to be held accountable for your actions and their consequences?

I swung all over the place in my thinking initially. From 'Sack them – make an example of them, gross misconduct'; to 'keep them working, they have not been tried and found guilty, so they are innocent until …' That seemed a bit ridiculous, as half the village had seen or heard the attacks. The team thought that we should stand by the boys wholeheartedly. I could find myself being swayed this way, until I thought of the victims, and some sense of need for justice for them.

The drive to the prison was in virtual silence, and pleasantries were short whilst we were there. James had shamed his community and they made that blatantly clear in their dealings with this ordinarily popular young man. Up until that point, I had been wholeheartedly convinced that my efforts to remove James from his potential assailant had been the right thing to do. For everyone. His brush-off was the first inkling I had that perhaps my efforts to save him might have been unwanted. I had sacrificed my own safety to keep him alive, yet he couldn't even bring himself to shake my hand. There's gratitude for you.

It took fifteen minutes to drive home; I did it with tears streaming down my cheeks. Some of them were tears of relief. Others were of the gradual recognition that perhaps I hadn't done this man a favour. He'd have run away. Instead, his 'boss' delivered him door to door to a jail sentence, that would lead to a trial, resulting in a fine he could not pay, for which his 'penance' would be conscription to the army. He didn't want to do that. He knew he couldn't stay in MK and had already made plans. He was going south, to start again in Uganda. A couple more days and he'd have been ready to go. Whatever my feelings on the justice angle of all this, I had scuppered James' chances of starting off elsewhere. It had not entered my thinking.

Wednesday 3rd January

We're back up to a private level 3, if public level 2. There was a big cattle raid near Aquem (20 miles) last night, bombing at Wedweil (40 ish miles) yesterday afternoon, and alleged word of PDF trouble north of Warawar (40+ miles) this morning. Bear in mind that 20 miles is many, many hours driving and many more footing, so sounds perhaps closer time-wise than it is. I was after a quiet office day, and have been here, there and everywhere. I had to call Shona and SFP team back from their trip to Wargeng for distribution – never nice to have to do that because you can't explain why on the radio, quite distressing to hear 'turn around and return to base'. Anyway, have seen the Commissioner, and received considerable 'reassurance' of the SPLA's strength, distance of the threat, and all round 'okeydokeyness' of the situation – and I was born yesterday!

Have just spoken to Fergus in Nairobi, he's back from his jollies. There he is trying to tell me about mince pies this, and nutritional survey that, and I'm trying to tell him without using any words of any real relevance that we're concentrating hard on security stuff, and not really in a position to give it max on the nutritional front. Add to that a 2 out of 5 quality reception, and you've got the makings of a rather unsatisfactory conversation. Telling Fergus would do nothing to improve our situation here, it's just nice to tell someone though. I've resorted to my classics CD again – I am growing up fast this year. I don't know, since leaving 2000 behind, I seem to be ageing unnaturally fast, I think I'd wear slippers if I had some.

Those were the days of my life

That was my Christmas 2000 – incredible days. It's like an exceptional film to look back on now. Grief, birth, despair, exhaustion, humour, fear, anger, joy, hope – so much life in such a short time.

During that period I think I developed a slightly better understanding of God, certainly of what and who God isn't, and what he doesn't do! He did not seem to shield me from any of it. Being challenged. Being hurt. Feeling despair. When I became a Christian, I thought I might be picking up an 'easier ride' ticket. Being on the same side as the 'Lord of All' would have one or two fringe benefits! But he doesn't seem to cushion the sharp edges.

There's a passage in Isaiah where the Lord is talking and says:

Fear not, for I have redeemed you;
I have summoned you by name; you are mine.
When you pass through the waters, I will be with you;
and when you pass through the rivers, they will not sweep over you.
When you walk through the fire, you will not be burned;
    the flames will not set you ablaze.
For I am the Lord, your God, the Holy One of Israel, your Saviour

          (Is. 43:1-3)

The waters, rivers and fire were still there. I think had God sat me down and spoken to me on 13th December 2001 in the way he did to Isaiah, he could well have said:

Don't worry, I have delivered you.
I am with you Emma, I have called you.
When the bombing planes circle, bombs will not drop.
When you pray in desperation, I will hear your prayers.
When you start getting too comfy, I will stretch you
When you touch death, I will comfort you.
When you are frightened, it will not consume you.
When you are far from your family, I will help you feel closer.
When the cook abandons you, Christmas dinner will still be a treat.
When you feel alone, I will provide company.
When you eat cake the rats have danced on, you will be able to enjoy it.
When you are confronted with loss, I will show you your role.
When you feel weak and unable, I will sustain you.
When you swim in the river, you will not fall sick.
When you laugh inappropriately, I will forgive you – again!

When you need to make decisions, I will be with you.
When there is insecurity, you will not be hurt.
Where there is joy, you will laugh.
When you see just one side of a coin, I will gently show you another.
When your mind is racing, I will let you sleep.
I am your Lord, your God, your Saviour – I am with you.

Leaving Mike Kilo

It was decided that, after three years, the project should close at the end of February due to improved nutritional conditions in the area. Close down was a spectacular effort of handing over and farewell dos. The majority of the team flew out of Mike Kilo on 26th February, whilst two of us drove one of the vehicles further south to another Tearfund project site.

It was an incredible journey.

Friday 2nd March

I'm in NBO. Let me give you just a brief resume of our anticipated 16 hour journey overland to Rumbek. 430km. Not far really, 5 or 6 hour drive at home.

1, After 6 hours driving we got stuck axle deep in river sand – having unpacked a lot of the trailer, and dug out the wheels we ended up laying out the tents we were carrying and driving out over them to get out of it.

2, Got across the river to find we had a flat tyre. Changed it only to find 1 of our other 2 spares had a slow puncture. 1 spare left.

3, The bearings went on the trailer. The wheels would periodically jam and could only be released if we reversed and then moved on forward again – slowly.

4, Got to our overnight stop at an NGO's compound 5 hours later than anticipated (4 hours later than curfew) – at 10:30pm, 11 hours on the road.

5, Day 2; swapped a dud tyre for a good one with our NGO hosts – which was nice!

6, Bolt by bolt our axle hub cracked.

7, An emergency Blue Peter sticky tape repair job worked for 3 hours until the last bolt pinged.

8, We removed the rear axle drive shaft (before it fell out), so were driving on forward wheel drive only with a placcy bag protecting the 'hole' where the axle hub should be – slower progress.

9, Didn't go 'round a roundabout' in a town 'the right way'. There was no roundabout, (actually there wasn't much of a town really) but that apparently was not the point. Detained by the police for over an hour.

10, Got to Rumbek at 10pm after 1ᶠ hours flat out driving at about 30km hour. Absolutely exhausted, cracking trip. Drank Coca-Cola from the UN compound. Lots.

Already shattered by the weeks building up to close down, the plan was simple; three drivers, including our local driver – Mading, a clear route and a realistic timeframe. The theory – get us, the vehicle, the trailer and contents to Rumbek as comfortably and easily as possible – no problem. The practice – twenty-seven hours on the road, eight hours of that was in the dark. By the time we parked up we were hardly able to speak because of tiredness, we couldn't turn our heads for the constant jarring and wrenching our necks had had on the twisting, potholed bush roads, and we were in a plodding mentality.

One thing that didn't make it into the diary happened at the end of the first day's driving. Moving forwards until the trailer wheels jammed, and backwards to release, forwards, and so on, progress was painfully slow. It was clear that we'd fallen a long way behind schedule, and could either spend the night in the bush, or try to get to this compound that was expecting us. We pushed on. Not lost, but certainly not knowing where we were. Nothing in sight other than the dark, inky blue horizon of land meeting sky, and the grasses, bushes, potholes and trees caught by the beams of the headlights. We were struggling – the vehicle, the trailer, the people – all struggling. Conversation had dried up hours before – the driver was concentrating on the road, the one in the back was resting, the passenger (me) was keeping an eye on the trailer.

As ever in the passenger seat, I felt myself beginning to nod off. Fighting to stay awake with Ben as he drove, I started to whistle. Whistling turned to song and I found the song books we'd used for our last morning devotions earlier that day – they'd been flung in the glove box. I sang and sang. I went through the book from start to end singing any of the praise and worship songs I knew.

When Ben knew the words, he'd join in. If he didn't, he'd whistle. If he didn't know the tune, he'd beat out the rhythm on the steering wheel. If he didn't know the rhythm, he just banged the steering wheel anyway! We must have done this for at least a couple of hours. I wasn't just singing for singing's sake. If I was going to do that I'd have dug into my sizeable repertoire of 'hits of the eighties'. It was an act of prayer too, an act of spontaneous prayer. In the thick of situations like that, I get a perspective on how helpless I am. I don't think it was a 'please God nothing else to go wrong, please', prayer. I think it was more of an acknowledgement, in the absolute stillness of the world, of God's vastness, his majesty.

As we sang, in the distance I saw something that momentarily terrified me. For the twenty minutes or so until we reached it, my eyes roamed along it, but never left the breathtaking sight. As far as I could see each side of the road, a line of fire. Fire is a tool of conflict in Sudan. That was my first thought. We were heading for a line of 'enemy fire'. Can you be peacefully scared? That's how I felt. Ben kept driving – I kept singing. Just as we approached the blaze Mading stirred in the back, 'grass burning, preparing the land for crops'. Of course – friendly fire.

We'd reached a song called *Be Still for the Presence of the Lord*.

I didn't alter the speed I was singing at, Ben didn't alter the speed he was driving at. I felt the heat of the burning grasses either side of the road as we started the second verse. I was singing the second line, which refers to the Lord burning with holy fire, as we drove through the fire. Pure coincidence? That takes a lot of faith in coincidence! Of all the songs, of all the times …

Incredible trip. Glad to have done it. Would I do it again? Perhaps once is enough – we'd run out of sticky tape!

Chapter 9

Working with the 'Other Side'

Summer in the UK, again! This year I had a home to go to. Admittedly I didn't exactly walk through the door to be bowled over by familiar comforts I loved. As far as interior furnishings went, my possessions totalled a large wicker chair, a wine rack, a footstool and a standing lamp. There was only one thing for it – Ikea.

Within the first couple of days I had become the owner of a bed, a chest of drawers, a sofa bed, a bookcase, a mattress, buckets for indoor plants and a myriad of left-over bits from various self-assembly items that didn't seem to go anywhere. Home did indeed become 'sweeter home' quickly.

★ ★ ★ ★

I'd left Sudan exhausted and, having had a few 'epilepsy-esque' symptoms, the Tearfund medical advisor and I thought a check-up seemed a good idea. I drove off to my nearest practice. In fear of sounding like my parents, I'll risk noting that the doctor I saw seemed to be 'a very young man indeed'. It wasn't his age that put me off – what got my back up was his ridiculously patronising comments, every time I'd respond to one of his questions about the last few months in Sudan.

'I was working on a nutrition project.'

'Oh, you poor thing.'

'It was the dry season so temperatures were exceptionally high.'

'Oh, you poor thing.'

Becoming increasingly exasperated, I thought of experimenting:

'My name's Emma and I'm in your surgery.'

'Oh, you …'!

The doctor informed me that, following the symptoms I'd had, I shouldn't be driving – for at least the next twelve months! He was not hearing me. So many epilepsy symptoms are shared with other states of health whose causes were highly possible in an extreme environment like Sudan. I mean:

Loss of peripheral vision – dehydration?

Incoherent thought processes – high levels of fatigue? Stress?

Bit of a head rush – excessive heat?

If a non-epileptic feels the above, they rest. If I feel the above, even with no way of proving any relationship directly to epilepsy – I lose my licence for a year! I get frustrated that the consequences of a couple of wobbly days are so dramatic and I get particularly bothered when the medic concerned will not take into account any extenuating circum- stances. I was now apparently in no fit state of health to drive home. As graciously as I could, I asked the doctor how exactly he suggested I was supposed to get myself and the car home. He didn't know. I drove, parked the car, put the keys away, went out and bought a bike!

* * * *

James from DRT UK called and asked whether I'd consider filling in as the Technical Services Officer for a few weeks. Although I do know my Phillips screwdriver from my pliers, can sing my way through the phonetic alpha- bet and can use a bottle jack, my techy knowledge stretches little further. Assisting the field teams with various problems and issues about solar power systems, vehicle quandaries and satellite phone dysfunctions wouldn't play to my strengths ... I took the job. I started work at the end of April and enjoyed the three months I was in the office – especially the team. Four of them had been my team mates in the field at different times, others had vis- ited on various assignments and others still were the voices I'd called from the field with requests of varying natures, or the faces I'd meet on my way to and from assignments.

* * * *

Sa finished her Burundi assignment and returned home. We spent five days transforming the still minimalistly furnished, magnolia throughout flat into a home. Pictures were framed, plants placed and blinds hung. It was a fantastic effort.

The summer of 2001 was the first time Sa and I lived in the flat together.

It was a bit of a gamble, the whole house-buying and housemate thing. In the two years since we'd travelled out to Kosovo, though, we'd seen each other act in and react to an incredible diverse portfolio of situations. I had no reason to suspect this friend of mine would be a lousy choice of housemate. I still haven't. I'm sure loads of people never let stocks of loo roll drop below sixteen; and it can't be all that uncommon to have marmite and banana together on toast; and not knowing that water and electricity cause a tiny fire hazard when they come into contact with one another – details, details! Joking aside, no complaints.

There are surely few friends who would offer to pay my share of the mortgage when my job possibilities looked sparse. Few who can get away with absent-mindedly telling their non-driving buddy that I should become a 'bus driver' because she saw an ad on a bus. Not many who would think to divert to my nieces' house 'on the way home' from Cornwall because she knows I couldn't do that right now. Less still who seem to understand my unspoken as well as my spoken thoughts. But that's Sa – something of a soul-mate, not merely a housemate.

* * * *

Tearfund were on the cusp of putting together some work in Afghanistan that I was interested in. However, several rounds of conversation between personnel, myself and a medical advisor came to the disappointing, sensible conclusion that until my disruptive brain patterns had settled, the rigours of Afghanistan were unsuitable for me. This issue of parts of the world and projects being inaccessible to me because of my health was hard to grapple with. I tend to have quite an optimistic streak: once I've had a sniff of an opportunity like that, I'm as good as there. It takes some hearty tugging to earth myself back on the ground again.

I still felt very strongly that I wanted to be doing relief work with Tearfund. At the time, the only other opening DRT had was in Serbia. This did not excite me. Having been working alongside Kosovo Albanians for ten months, my view of Serbia and more particularly the Serb people was not a positive one. I'm not at all proud of my anti-Serb prejudice. But I do understand where it came from. To hear one side of any conflict for that length of time and see the extent of the suffering caused is bound to leave an impression. Whilst I was considering taking the Serbia post I felt a sense of disloyalty to the Kosovo staff that we worked with. I prayed about it.

Gradually over the summer my view changed. How could I, as a Christian, profess to show love to all people, if my actions ruled some people out? Eventually, I got to the point that almost *because* I had been in Kosovo I felt I should go. Jesus' commission was not to 'go and make disciples of all nations you judge to be worthy', but to go to 'all nations', prejudices regardless.

I accepted the post.

Serbia 2001–02 'We have to say goodbye so we can say hello again'

Monday 3rd September 2001

Sunday hurt. It had been Kate's fifth birthday party. The party had finished, my bags were packed, knowing glances exchanged and with that Mum, Dad and I got up to leave. I put on my shoes sitting on the stairs. Kates leapt on my lap, flung her arms around my neck and squeezed, tightly. Eventually she let go, knelt on the floor with a pen and piece of paper. In her best 'turned five years old' handwriting she carefully wrote: I will miss you Aunty

XX

With that my valves opened, hot, wet tears surfaced and fell heavily. I tried to postpone them, to order them to wait until I was out of the house. I adamantly instructed my waterworks not to let the girls see me upset. They stubbornly disobeyed – they kept rolling out of my lids, coursing down my cheeks and following the route gravity had for them.

Two year old Bex then held my face in both of her hands, looked me straight in the eye and adamantly stated:

'Em, no plane. No plane.'

The power of speech left me then, as it has now – more tears fall as I type. I held them both in my arms, inanely smiling from one to the other through an undisguised veil of sadness. Sara and Andy plucked them gently from my neck, we kissed, I hugged my big sister and she held me tight and told me she loved me, I loved her back but was unable to articulate it, we walked out of her home and drove off. I don't remember how far we'd got down the M4 but as I lay down to sleep, still my goodbye tears fell.

Another goodbye. I am incredibly close to both my nieces and in spite of the fact that I've spent most of their short lives working overseas, Sara and Andy have done a wonderful job of keeping me in their thoughts in my absence. Since Kates has been old enough to speak – and in recent years with Bex too – theirs is the goodbye I have found the most painful. As adults we seem to lose that forthright honesty that children have. We don't say 'don't go', as we know the person has to and that it will grieve them to hear our words, so we put a lid on them, hug firmly, wish the person well and let them go. Kates and Bex still have the uninhibited freedom of their childhood to say it as it is.

Last time I left home for Sudan at the end of my two week R&R in the UK, the rest of the family were clearing away the dishes, whilst I sat explaining to the then four year old Kates that I was flying out the next day.

'Why do you have to go back, Aunty? I want you to stay.'

'There are lots of children over there in our village who are hungry, Kates, and we have to try and give them some food.'

She paused and moved her carrots round her plate.

'I get hungry sometimes, can't you stay here and help me too?'

I'm sure my tears come directly from my heart at times like that, like a wound. A flesh wound sheds blood; an emotional one – involuntary tears fall instead.

'Yes, but Mummy gives you food from the cupboards and the fridge, doesn't she?'

'Not always, sometimes she says I have to wait until tea time.'

How can you argue with that!? I changed tack.

'I'll see you in three months.'

'When's that?'

'That's the end of spring when the flowers have all come out, OK?'
'OK.'

She snuggled up and we both sat, wondering how soon the flowers would be out.

I'm very well aware that in many ways I have an incredibly privileged lifestyle, an awful lot of 'pros', with opportunities to go places, meet people, experience different cultures and do a job I believe in. But the cost to me after three plus years of this lifestyle, the 'cons' – or certainly the most significant – is dipping out for months at a time of the lives of those I love at home. Sure, you get to hear of the high highs and the lowest of the lows, but the day-to-day bits that shape a person rarely warrant a mention on the email and those are the bits that, for this short season in my life at least, I have accepted to do without.

I have loved what I have done with Tearfund, but that does not come cheaply, certainly not free. There is a cost. My cost is the pain, and it is pain, of separation from my family and friends; the pain of the goodbye conversations with my nieces. The only way to describe that is – pain. It does heal, but it hurts!

Finding my feet and not putting them 'in it'

Assignment number four; what was initially a five month contract evolved into nine months in Serbia, in Nis, the second or third town of Serbia. As a result of the last decade-plus of ethnic conflict in the Balkans, 750,000 Serbs have become refugees from Croatia and Bosnia and where no internationally recognised border has been crossed i.e. from Kosovo, they bear the title of 'internally displaced persons' (IDPs). 750,000 extra people have been absorbed by a country still paying the cost of sanctions, the aftermath of war, into a once prosperous economy that has taken a significant tumble. Tearfund were predominantly addressing shelter needs – the lack of suitable accommodation to house the Croatian, Bosnian and Kosovo Serbs who had by perceived necessity left their homes. We were working in southern Serbia with people living both in Collective Centres – properties that to a greater or lesser extent had been adapted in order to become habitable – former factories, offices and schools and also in private accommodation – homes where owners had allowed families to stay with them for rent, for free or for payment in kind. In the Collective Centres we'd survey properties, assess living conditions and contract out recommended works to construction firms. For families living in private accommodation, again we'd assess and survey and, in liaison with the hosted and host family, would supply materials and technical expertise to help families carry out the work themselves.

I was joining the team at the start of Phase two of the programme, the others in the expat team had worked together on Phase one. A springbok, a kiwi and three roses – three English 'girls' and the two 'boys' from the Colonies! A translator's nightmare regarding the various accents floating around. Gary was from South Africa, the team leader or programme director. New Zealander Mike was the logistics co-ordinator. Ann, Vranje's field co-ordinator from Croydon, was the closest geographically that any of us were to the epicentre of the Queen's English! Jude was the programme support manager from Birmingham and her dulcet Brummy tones seemed directly proportional to how tired she was. These were to be my colleagues, my playmates, my church and my housemates for the next few months. We worked together, ate together, played together, prayed together and brushed our teeth together. My first impression was a positive one. My job title was field co-ordinator – Nis. My task was to co-ordinate the work of a team of nine local project staff, including engineers, social workers, logisticians and a project administrator.

Tuesday 4th September
My 1st day, day two of orientation. A completely new national staff team have been recruited for this project. Conversation began.
'Your first visit to the Balkans?'
'No, I worked in Kosovo for 10 months.'
'Oh, where?'
'Gjakove.'
'No – that is Drakovica.'

Heck. My first (known) Albanian/Serb cultural cock-up, referring to the town I knew as my home for 10 months by its Albanian name – to a Serb. There are going to be many more of those to come, I'm sure. My mastery of the Albanian language was pitifully small, limited to greetings and knowing the names of items such as tiles, timber and bricks. Having not spoken any Albanian for over a year, only now does it resurface – at the most inappropriate moment! I don't yet know how the temperature of animosity lies between these two historically opposed ethnic groups. I guess that will become clearer as time goes by.

I falteringly struck up another conversation.
'Have you lived here all your life?'
'No I'm from Kosovo – an IDP, I had to flee from Pristina, my Albanian neighbours were going to kill me.'
Another challenge to what I know, or rather have grown to believe as truth. The Albanians were the victims – the Serbs, the perpetrators. Well, this Serb for one was not a perpetrator, at least, not at that time, in that place.

Wednesday 5th September
I'm sitting here with the stove out of arms reach as I'm having a session of culinary experimentation. One of those times that separates the genii of the kitchen from those banned from entering. We had chicken for dinner and, inspired by the lack of wastage cast out as junk, I'm making soup. It has taken a trip away from home on another assignment to dabble with the chicken carcass and left over veg with random herbs and spice soup.

Strange to visit my first Serb homes. These were special cases identified by the municipality as needing desperate assistance; refugees and IDPs living in spare rooms of host families.
The first home had a sagging ceiling – most of the homes in Kosovo had no ceiling (or roof). The second had no internal bathroom – in Kosovo even the houses we'd refurbished had an external loo. The third had only a concrete floor, not floorboards – in Kosovo a quality mud floor was good enough.

A real slap in the face for me over of the importance of not directly comparing the needs of these different people groups. I heard a story from a Serb family of a son lost fighting in Kosovo, yet I clearly remember the eyes of an old Kosovo Albanian telling me of his two missing sons, the rape of his grand daughters, the torture of his brother and the torching of his home. Relative loss. Relative needs. The Serbs have lost much – but theirs seems to be on a different scale of tragedy from that of the Kosovo Albanians. But again, the loss of the Kosovo Albanians is different from that of the southern Sudanese. I know this but need to transfer it from head to heart fast, otherwise my compassion will run dry and without it, co-ordinating this project cold will not be on.

There it is again, as it was when I moved from Sudan to Kosovo, the direct comparison of people group to people group, with me acting as impulsive judge and jury as to how much they have a, suffered and b, need and – dare I admit it – deserve support. At least I was aware I was doing it this time and knew to an extent how I needed to counter it – meet people, individual people and hear their story, catch a glimpse of their lives; lose the anonymity of the collective impersonalised umbrella.

Friday 7th September
One of those beautiful, exquisite, precious days that blesses you with all of the riches of this work and none of the trash. We had a project team workshop on construction standardisation and need prioritisation – we started the day with coffee and a kicking discussion on what we are going to do within this project, what we can and what we can't do – how to keep it equitable from one beneficiary family to the next. Brilliant – the team has flown through 'forming', raced through norming, bypassed storming and here we are, on day five, performing! Common goal, shared vision, unity in purpose, mutual respect for different strengths, we're off like Christie from the blocks!

We went out in the villages visiting a few refugee/IDP families and assessing their living conditions. One house was home to three families, three generations. They fled from Kosovo in May 1999, forced to flee under threat of death in Pristina from their Kosovo Albanian neighbours. Now living with no water, tumble down pit latrine, cranky doors that don't fill the frame, two rooms in total, no bathroom/washing area. The team concluded that within our criteria, budget, time and personnel constraints we will be able to:

- Partition the big room – hence a room for each family
- Connect up mains water
- Provide materials for a new latrine
- Provide new doors, replace cracked windows
- Insulate the floor
- Install a basic bathroom

This is exactly what it's about, having the privilege of practically assisting people living in a sub-standard environment. Not their fault, nor their failing, they were getting on with lives but happened to be wearing the wrong ethnic label, in the wrong place two years ago and their lives were turned upside down. What we're doing is not about building walls, it's also partly about hope and pride and the future being brighter than the past.

Watching the national teams' faces today was a treat as they got increasingly excited by the project ahead. They've told me at length of their felt guilt and shame of the crimes their nation has committed – 'but we could do nothing.' They felt powerless to stop the tide of wrongs their leader was authorising. Dasic, my project manager, a 40 something year old, mild-mannered gentleman and engineering professional, spoke and as he did, his eyes filled with a welter of still raw emotions, guilt, shame, anger at being used, bitterness towards Milosevic. The passion the team have for using their skills genuinely to assist their fellow Serbs is evident. This commitment shone through so clearly today as they discussed recommendations and chatted with the families. Brilliant. Other than me, the project team are all national staff – it's their project for their people. I'm merely a participating guest – like it.

September 11th 2001

Tuesday 11th September

Walked back to the hotel with the two consultants to find that, in the words of CNN, 'America is at war with an unknown enemy.' Horrific footage. Horrific tragedy. Initial local reaction by a few on the ground here seem to be along the lines of 'Now you know what it feels like to be on the receiving end of tragedy.' Naturally this response was swiftly surpassed by shock, empathy and sympathy, but once again my comfortable apolitical blinkers are lifted fractionally. The ramifications of this catastrophe are going to be huge. Such a low tech, yet incredibly meticulous act of logistics – sometimes reality seems more fanciful than science fiction.

Thursday 13th September
Email after email from friends and family are coming in with news of the events and aftermath in the US. I feel like I'm in a bubble – I have not had chance to buy a paper, go online, I haven't got my radio and the flat I've been staying in has no telly. Very bizarre to hear of reactions back home, yet be so isolated from perhaps the most horrific deliberate act of terrorism in peace times. The conspiracy theories are being speculated on here. I found it perplexing today to drive past building after building that the US obliterated two years ago as legitimate targets and yet simultaneously feel appalled by the events of Tuesday. The contexts, motives, etc, are admittedly incomparable, but the outcome – loss of life, tragedy and disruption are where the similarities lie.

The ripples September 11th sent around Serbia were smaller by far, it seems, than those in the UK. Cocooned as I was from the rife speculation and talk of secondary immediate strikes, the belief that the USA's little sister Britannia was next in line resulted in a strong feeling of separation from those at home. I felt it particularly acutely because it's taken as read that whenever you leave on assignment, you are putting yourself at a level of increased risk, more than those who are left at home and certainly that you face different if not greater risks. So for the UK, for home, to seem vulnerable was disturbing.

It shook me. Not so much the event itself, nor the news broadcasts of it, but the number of friends who immediately got in contact. Messages varied from factual accounts of the event, 'getting in touch' contact from people who normally wouldn't get in touch, to circular prayers and notes expressing fear. The magnitude of the impact seemed in many ways disproportionate to the scale of the event itself. What it signified, however, was what hit harder. Other than those immediately involved who had lost loved ones, it was the wake up call that the tragedy gave that left a bigger mark. Terrorism on an unprecedented scale had moved from science fiction to fact. Not another predictable news report from the Middle East or Northern Ireland, but innocent people going about their lives in the very heart of the most powerful nation in the world had taken a hit.

As the hours, days and weeks passed and no other major attacks occurred, it gently slipped away and my concern faded that there would be a secondary strike, particularly in the UK.

Tuesday 18th September
'I was disgusting this morning.'
Dasic's words took me by surprise during a serious, heavy, techy meeting about the proposed scopes of works for the collective centres.
'I'm sorry?' I replied.
Back came the stone faced confirmation 'I was disgusting with the team this morning'.
A little floored by this, I took the time to nod gently, tilt my head and stroke my eyebrow thoughtfully. The penny dropped – 'discussing'! Nice one. My giggle was swallowed away, my smile contained and my desperate laughing eyes diverted from his. We went on.

Thursday 20th September

We were reading Romans today. I think it was chapter 12(ish) and it finished with the verse 'do not be overcome by evil, but overcome evil with good'. Bin Laden's name is audible from the lounge as I type and I feel I'm looking around the world at the news at the mo seeing again and again a mess of hate, mistrust, revenge, anger, fear – and it's grim, isn't it? It's frightening. I don't have the answers, I don't know how the US is supposed to overcome terrorism 'with good', but surely a lethal and sudden strike cannot be the best way forward.

WWJD? What Would Jesus Do? If he, Jesus, were here walking the earth on September 11th, what would his reaction have been? If Jesus was Blair or Bush what would his response be?

Would he strike back? Doubt it.

Sanctions? Don't think so.

Nothing? Surely not.

I can't see that our God who allowed himself to be stripped, beaten and crucified would go for retaliation. BUT, equally I can't see that he'd do nothing. So where does that leave us? What are the choices? – 'overcome evil with good'; if not war, then what? Do you rebuke and forgive? Can we, or should we, ever justify war? If you'd had the buttons of American military, financial, political muscle at your finger tips, which ones would you have pressed?

Thankfully the buttons at my finger tips tend – at their most powerful – to be for the telephone or remote control – but I'm growing in awareness that I cannot afford to walk blind, with my hands over my ears shouting 'I can't hear you, I'm not listening' through some of these bigger issues. As I live neither at Number 10, nor in that big White House it's not my responsibility to get it right; but it is my responsibility to be informed, to develop a level of understanding, to move from my current physically uncomfortable, yet mentally easy, unopinionated, grey, fence-straddling seat. Jesus' circles included the politicians, his religion didn't exclude them, he was challenged for example on the rights and wrongs of paying taxes to Caesar (Lk. 20). I can't imagine Jesus saying 'Well, I'm not sure. It's a right mess isn't it? I don't know.' There is nothing in the Bible that leads me to believe that Jesus was a fluffy, 'whatever' guy and as such his disciples have to follow suit. It's a shame he didn't leave a little book of answers to some of these trickier situations.

Prejudice

Friday 5th October

Incredible. A teacher who works for the partner organisation was at the workshop today. She was led outside her school yesterday and grades 7&8 children were allegedly encouraged to beat her because of her evangelical Christian faith. Her colleagues requested that the children did this. When we talk about persecution at home, we talk about disinterest, we talk about people saying 'whatever's right for you, but I'm fine', we talk about a degree of awkwardness if you 'say grace' or give thanks before dinner, or some friends thinking you've become a bit of a religious fruitcake. That's British persecution in my experience. Here, an able teacher, not proselytising to her pupils, doing her job, is verbally humiliated by her colleagues in front of 200 children and physically abused.

'Where were you the night of………….?'

To mark the one year anniversary of Milosevic's downfall, I was bobbing up and down in the shadow of a massive bronze statue of a man on a horse, to the pulsating din of Serbia's top bands, in the main square in Belgrade. There you go, one I didn't expect. Apparently in the days and weeks preceding Milosevic's exit, throughout the night crowds of 50,000+ people, whistle-blowing and marching, would mass in Belgrade in peaceful yet powerful demonstrations against the authorities. These marches would inevitably spill over into clashes with the police, until eventually the people realised they were no longer at the mercy of their leaders. The subsequent raid on Milosevic's place resulted in his arrest – and Serbia's liberation from their infamous leader. The atmosphere last night was buzzing; youths, young families, old men, all out, telling their story of this time, together on the streets again but this time in victory, in historical celebration following 365 days of change, of more hope, of this big new chapter.

Sunday 21st October

Prejudice. I got challenged on that last week by Dasic – my anti-Serb prejudice on arrival here. I've been stewing off and on about it this week, defending my position, justifying my thoughts and attitudes in my head and have finally reached the grand old conclusion that ... well ... he was right.

I knew before I came out here that I'd find it hard, having had 10 months with Kosovo-Albanians, hearing their stories, living through their recovery, seeing their lives torn apart, touching their grief. What I didn't know was that my heart on this matter would be so visibly on my sleeve. Dasic recounted my first sentence to the team when I arrived; 'I'm English and you are Serbs.' I meant it along the lines that we're different, language differences, culture differences, etc. but what he and the rest of the team heard was 'I'm English and you are the perpetrators of horrific crimes.'

I don't deny that that is how I felt – it's true. But now, a couple of months down the line, I've kicked myself for putting all this in such small, neat boxes. Albanians = goodies, Serbs = baddies. I'm not trying to say that what Serbia did to Kosovo was right. It wasn't. I am saying that this man, this Serbian engineer (with his uncanny knack of offering me gum at stressy times) is not necessarily guilty, nor worthy of my judgement. That this mother of four, roasting her peppers and harvesting her grapes, is not necessarily a depraved, inhumane being. That the child playing with his basketball is being schooled to regard Albanians as a sub class, beneath Serbs.

Every now and then I catch myself looking at people, trying to guess whether they torched that house in Cok that the old man lived in; whether they played a part in taking captive Bekim's cousin, or cutting off the arm of the guy in Orahovac. Someone did those things. I want to write to the team here at some point, I want to articulate all this; I want them to know what I saw in Kosovo, what I heard, I want them to know why my attitudes formed. But I want them to know too that some of those attitudes have been turned upside-down as these 'baddies' have become my colleagues, my neighbours and my friends.

Towards the end of the programme in Kosovo, a 'needs assessment' team from the UK office went into Serbia for an initial recce. There was

amongst the Kosovo team – myself included – a real unmasked reluc-
tance to consider initiating a programme across the border. The level of
animosity between the two people groups seemed to be huge. I've heard
many tales of forgiveness and reconciliation, particularly amongst
Rwandan Hutus and Tutsis following the genocide of '94, but I could
not envision Kosovo Serbs and Albanians getting to that point. Maybe
it's a time factor. Maybe this is all too soon, I hope so. The doubt I have
is that history seems to run so deep in the Balkans and people know
their history. If a visitor came to the UK, my historical tour of the Great
British Isles would be pretty patchy – and probably include as much of
Robin Hood and King Arthur as it would the more traditional material! In Serbia the whole team seemed able to tell me 'who fought whom,
where and when'. Phenomenal. Trouble is, you go back x years and such
and such a piece of land belonged to the Albanians, go back further and
it belonged to the Serbs, further – Albanians, etc. So trying to come to
some sort of conclusion seems impossible. I was trying to talk Katy
through this sort of thing last week (tricky subject when you're five, but
she did ask). She seemed to understand it, so I asked her what should
happen. Her adamant response came quickly:

'England and Wales should have the land and everything on it, then
they wouldn't fight'!

Colonial Empire resurgence in the next generation?

In the swing of things

Sunday November 25th
Mike and I sat in here reading our Bibles separately this morning and
have agreed that a fine big screen picture could be produced. We'd last
about five minutes before one would 'hmph!' shake their heads and say
'Listen to this, right.....'. He was on heads being thrown over city walls,
concubines being locked up, seemingly arbitrary and inconsistent forgiveness of wrongdoers. I was reading about Samson and have found the
phrase of all biblical phrases so far. The gist is that Samson is letting his
hair down ('cos he did have a lot of the stuff) at his pre-wedding do and

set a riddle to the guests with a wager on it. The guests, fearful of losing, threatened Samson's betrothed with death if she did not tell them the answer. So…. the guests got the riddle right and Samson realised that he'd been betrayed by his potential good lady. He was livid and 'burnt with anger'; he said to the guests:

'If you had not ploughed with my heifer,
You would not have solved the riddle.

I love it. I guess 'messed with my girl' is the contemporary equivalent. You 'ploughed with my heifer' – wonderful phrase! Mike is looking for opportunities to use it this coming week.

The snow is still coming on down outside. Mike is sitting with a permanent marker making draughts pieces for the game I inadvertently said yes to. Very Blue Peter. Jude is shouting gently at the cat 'get out and I'll feed you, stay in and I won't.' The flapjack is ready for the oven – guesstimates all round (on ingredients as well as quantities). We couldn't get oats, so we're using Alpen – course it'll work!

The heat limited play times in Sudan. The lack of it over the winter months largely dictated our options in Serbia. That said, I got close to having a balanced work, rest and play life. Mike, Jude and Gary were all hugely involved in this. It's fairly rare to be living and working with three other people who are all so 'up for it' leisure wise. The clay court tennis club across the river in town was welcoming and hospitable. Many were the blood pressure lowering shots belted across the net from time to time. When the outside courts were coated in snow, there was 'the bubble' with its fantastic acoustic sounds.

I was given a mini table tennis table as a Christmas present that made its way out across Europe. It was great. About two and a half feet long and over a foot in width. There were some serious matches on that table. As skill levels improved – play was taken increasingly seriously. It became much more than a game. Stakes were high – we played for chocolates, or exemption from doing the dishes – things that mattered. Losers' strops were all too common. Laps of honour and victory dances were not rare. At one stage I was so gripped by the Titanic ping-pong struggle I was engaged in, that when a telephone call from the UK came from someone who apparently had had to spend quite a while getting a line my abrupt response was – 'Can you call back in five minutes? I'm mid-game'. Tragically I went on to lose that match, the chocolate and nearly my respect for Gary as he danced his way around the room victoriously! Fortunately the caller got through again to me once the post-match dust had settled and the disappointment had worn off.

Three hours down the road, round the corner and up through the mountains was the Kaponik ski resort. Mike and Gary both had quite a substantial amount of experience of wearing long slippery surfaced planks strapped to their feet, on white slippery stuff, whilst on a slippery gradient. Jude, Ann and I? – not so. The boys demonstrated gracious and undeserved levels of patience with us as we slid, stumbled and swerved during those first few Sundays on the slopes. The ski lifts in particular provided ample opportunity for demonstrations of ineptness and inexperience, usually with a queue behind us whilst the assistant was required to assist frequently.

We slid, stumbled and swerved

Photo: Gary Swart

Efforts were made to get out of the office at a reasonable time and, without any effort at all, we managed not to get into work in the mornings before necessary! Certainly we worked hard – and play? Quite committed to that too.

Tuesday 27th November
Petrovac Collective Centre is now ... signed off! Another one completed – bring it on! Great day, flip high highs and low lows in the working world this week, don't know how much more of this despair (yesterday) and elation (today) I can take. We spent an hour and a half checking it out, witnessing the effects that new windows, a new roof, new floor, paintwork, infestation treatment etc have had on that place and those people. They are warmer, more comfortable, their toilets flush, their showers are hot – oh man. Money well spent. Nigel was with me and the whole engineering team of four decided they were up for it, plus the Commissioner of Refugees, two reps from the Contractor, two Directors of the Centre Board and two members of the press. Unbeknownst to me, I conducted an off-the-cuff interview – I thought I was having a friendly chat, before I realised the newspaper journalist was getting everything down on paper!

Amazing changes, not just in the building. The Commissioner of Refugees was, by all accounts, incredibly difficult to work with last project, but at the end of the sign-off, he was so delighted he invited all 12 of us for lunch – on him! We accepted – it was lunch time after all! Conversation spanned the usual eclectic mix of round the table chit-chat – Afghanistan, football, long term policy for Serbian future, the best fish in the river, whether any donors would treat as priority the headmaster's declared need for a new gymnasium floor, how to make soft cheese, etc. Everyone had an opinion on everything, no-one knew very much about anything and we all knew that and enjoyed each other's company.

Back in the office Nigel had a meeting with my project team – without me. 'They are possibly the most contented team of staff I've ever met' – music to my ears. Gosh, of all the things he could have said, that probably lifts my heart and my attitude the most. The minor digs of last week are well and truly behind us and we seem to have clicked again. So important, so much else can fit around that.

Always encouraging that a corker of a day occurs when the boss from Teddington is out and about! It was great to see some tangible outcome of our work as we signed off that first completed Collective Centre. Most of the visible work – particularly with the private accommodation – took place from February onwards once the temperatures had started rising; so for much of the project, there was actually little to see as a result of our efforts. Tasks such as the installation of sewage outlets or electrical cabling can be time-consuming, yet visually very little changes. Laying floorboards or installing new windows and doors – all by necessity happens nearer the end and then you can hardly keep up to speed with the progress. So much time spent in preparation; preparing contracts, preparing tenders, preparing selection criteria, preparing assessment forms. All part of the process, but so little to see. I tend to be motivated by seeing at least some of the fruits of my labours as I go, rather than reaping a bumper harvest at the end.

Pastoral Weekend

Thursday 6th December
Unusual working day, well afternoon anyway. I spent the first part down at the police station trying to get a work visa – they still haven't quite granted me one from September 3rd.

We held an Alpha course type session after work today and threw it open to the staff – all of them came. Mike had put the talk together. It was one of those things where I'd made all the right supportive noises – yet did not actually lift any of my 10 digits to help. Not good. It was great, bit stiff to start with, but opened up big time. I realised how much my reasoning behind my faith has melted away. When I became a Christian I had to make a choice, based upon evidence and opinion, evaluating the facts and the gaps and coming to a conclusion. I did. Since then, I've lost a lot of my sharpness in understanding the reasons. The conclusion has remained intact, but I can now no longer present such a reasoned explanation of what it's all about. Cracking therefore to hear the guys' objections to Christianity:

Where was Jesus between ages 15–30?

Why, if Jesus preaches on one body, is the church so divided?

The teaching in the Bible is good, but nothing more, God doesn't have any other effect on our day to day lives.

Surely God's plan had gone awry, otherwise he would not have had to send and kill his only son.

It's interesting that the guys here are all so open to the reality of God and spiritual realms, as opposed to me who used to have absolute confidence that there couldn't possibly be a God. That made the rest of the Gospel hard to swallow!

Friday 7th December

Finished work early and were out by 12:30, heading for Kaponik and our 'pastoral weekend' by 13:30. Mike and I got here 1st and, pinnies on, set to with roasty dinner, Christmas decorations, roaring fire and mulled wine. It's beautiful, the world up here is white. Jude, Ann, Gary and Phil arrived at 7 ish from Belgrade and we ate. Phil is the Tearfund Pastor – very down to earth, but well up there in his passion – going to like him.

We spent a bit of time looking at where we've been in the last 5 years and writing what we'd like the next 5 years to look like. I realised how much my account of '96–'01 was made up of achievements, what I'd been doing where and with whom. It was career related stuff predominantly – with a couple of high and lowlights thrown in. But my '02–'07 'story' was maybe 10% on career. The shift in what is important to me was massive. It was about people, about relationships, trust, faith, joy, about doing what I can do best and am passionate about. I know these things are priorities in my life, yet I allow them to be squeezed, to be replaced by what society tells me is important. You know? When did 'society' last pat someone on the back for restoring damaged relationships, or taking leaps of faith in following God? No, it doesn't work like that, but a career path, a salary increase, an exotic holiday or achievement, that's where the points are. Quite a challenge – needs action. So I'll hand in my notice, work as a volunteer – maybe some more consideration first, eh!

Saturday 8th December
18:00pm: I'm sitting in a log cabin, on top of a beautiful mountain that could, with little imagination, be the subject of winter scene picture postcards. Logs are burning in the fire, the guys are chilling out, the tinsel is up and we've been for a walk through the forests – got cold, came home and drank mulled wine. What a privileged weekend.

I'm realising afresh as well quite what a good team this is. Looking around, Jude's in the kitchen, Gary's chopping wood, Ann's talking with Phil, Mike's working on his Ozzie accent and I'm typing this. Everything gets done, nothing gets missed, but we are able to chill out with each other. Just because one is working, all don't feel they should. Quite amazing in that way – so hassle and stress free.

The five of us sat around chatting probably for the first time in a long time, first time we've all been still enough in one place long enough to talk. So good, to be able to appreciate each other and enjoy each other. We've had a bedtime Baileys – no ice in the freezer. Nipped outside and brought in a two foot long icicle hanging off the gutter. Special times.

Monday 10th December
What a day! None of the monotony and predictability that accompany the mundane working life I fear falling into at some stage. I found myself today fighting a fire. I was writing a letter as we drove and I saw smoke ahead. Not a rare sight, there are lots of agricultural fires out here, but as we drove closer, I felt we should stop. We picked up the fire extinguisher in the vehicle and ran off the road to find a distraught couple of women running back and forth from their well to their outhouse, their barn which was burning like a bonfire. I sprayed the extinguisher. It was like aiming a water pistol at a volcano – it did nothing. The fire hadn't taken full grasp of the

building and it looked as though we might be able to do something if we were quick. We couldn't. The speed those flames devoured the building was incredible. The owner arrived back and my eyes met his in panic as we realised that his house, only metres from the barn, was at risk. There was a wooden fence and three small trees between the two buildings and the ferocity that furnace had was terrifying. The women wept as they worked, Dasic drew water from the well, the owner chopped down the trees one after the other and I cleared them away. We ripped apart the wooden fence and doused the ground between the two buildings. The heat was phenomenal – it was minus 9 Celsius, but we were down to one layer.

Eventually the fire engine arrived and the water showered on. The house was safe, the other buildings destroyed, but the house was safe. I had gone through incredible feelings of excitement. I have never been so involved and so close to something like that. Never been alongside a family in such an intense and real drama of blind anguish, fearing the loss of their home, disappearing literally up in smoke before their eyes. Were they lucky or unlucky? They lost their barn – but they kept their home. I don't know…

We drove on to sign off our 3rd collective centre. The owner was off his head on booze, which made his signature quite creatively varied on the 5 documents, but did make for trying conversations on the finer points of the works. A family at the centre turned on us. We'd knocked to go into their room and ask them if they were satisfied with the works. Foolish question . They are refugees and have been living in shabby dormitory accommodation, having lost their home, their possessions and their son in a war they wanted no part in –
'Are you pleased that your toilet now flushes and there is a spangley coat of paint on your walls?'
What was I expecting back?
'Oh yes, delighted, thank you for enhancing my wonderful life with your generous efforts and assistance.'
Sometimes I appal myself with my insensitivity and lack of understanding. What can you say to that family pulling out their hair, with little hope and little to look forward to?

The owner stepped in and had a glass of raki with the man. It seemed to pacify his anger, a temporary plaster for a permanent wound. It's important to remember that what we are doing out here is making a difference, even if it is not as big and for as many as we would wish — but it is a positive difference, without doubt.

Chapter 10

Even Though the Fighting has Stopped ...

Happy New Year

Saturday 5th Jan

We had a training day today on stress with a consultant from the UK. Fantastic, all 20 something of us on the programme going through stressors, symptoms and stress management techniques. The management team then had a session on debriefing. Good, good stuff and I'm so aware of how much difference quality and timely debriefs have made to me.

Out of antifreeze in the car this morning – not good. We limped with poor vision down to the training, nipping into every garage or car bits and bobs place on the way. Would you believe it, no-one has any! Winter is a relatively predictable phenomenon out here. Inspiration struck. Alcohol! Jude and I perused the shelves and selected the cheapest, strongest booze we could lay our hands on – Lemon Vodka! I confidently poured it in and no worries yet.

Sunday 6th Jan

Inspired by Eurosport's showing of the downhill slalom, we took to the slopes. Armed with three sledges, multi-layers, a camera and enthusiasm pouring out of our steaming nostrils – we plodded up the hill and up further, then we hit it. Fabulous. Like children we whooped and giggled, soared and collapsed time after time on the way back down to Gabrovac.

Friday 18th Jan

Have been challenged (so far not to the point of action, but it may be imminent), about how tight I am with my money, time, etc. and how little I put my money where my mouth or heart is. Many people assume that we make massive sacrifices to come and do this work. In some ways that's true – I've worn thermals for two months now, I've gone through withdrawal symptoms re. liberal use of the telephone, but in other ways, I'm a paid professional, doing what I enjoy, living conditions are fine, working with a great team, etc. Not on balance a life of horrific hardship, most of the time! So..... have been quite challenged on my giving, or rather lack of giving. 90% of the world's wealth in the hands of 10% of the population – I'm in that 10% and so to be fair is anyone reading this. I know I can't single handedly redress the global poverty problem, but I do have a responsibility to do my bit. 'When I have any money, I get rid of it as quickly as possible, lest it find a way onto my heart' (John Wesley). Well said, John.

Sunday 27th Jan

Teamwise, I have found it hard this week. A lot of big work decisions needing to be made. Team life shows you some of the potential rougher edges of relationships, some of the smoothest too. To work, rest and play harmoniously with the same few people, for months at a time, takes far more than a Mars bar! Great marriage prep!

One of the things that has grabbed me this year is the need for balance between selfishness and excessive selflessness! If there is someone always 'give give giving', that can be as hard, if not harder to deal with than if there is a 'take take taker' in the team. Otherwise, everyone always feels an unnecessary debt of gratitude to the giver, always owes them something; the giver feels like a martyr and no one's happy!

Monday 28th Jan

'It's my biggest high and my stressiest low, do you know what I mean?'
'Yup. It's marriage without the sex.'
We sat in the precinct café, enjoying the sunshine and nodding, Gary supping his cappuccino and me slurping my hot choc. My comment the

former, his the latter. I'd asked one of 'those' weighted questions: 'Gary, do you ever find it difficult when so and so does such and such?'
What I was actually saying was more along the lines of: 'It does my head in when so and so does such and such!'

He nodded, supped and chuckled – I think he knew what I was getting at. Good to get it said and not slip into that backstabbing, bad-mouthing place that you can't afford to let yourself get to when you're living 24/7 with the same few people. Hence the comment re marriage. He has a point.

Team life can surely be more intense than marriage. Admittedly the commitment to each other was for months rather than until death's parting; but it's rare for a husband and wife to work that closely together, probably rarer still to spend almost all of their social time together. It's incredible how many people – since we've been back – have commented on how 'close we seemed to be as a team', how much we 'enjoyed one another's company'. It's true and I believe that it didn't develop purely by chance or effortlessly. We worked at it. Sure, it helped that we got on well most of the time, but by no stretch of the imagination did we have perpetual working and domestic bliss. It seemed to be how we handled the times when bliss was absent that made the difference. We were committed to each other and to making 'us' work.

Prayer seems to have been our biggest weapon in this. We prayed a lot. There seems to be a level of honesty, integrity and intimacy demanded and developed with people you spend time praying with, that cuts deeper than non-prayer based relationships and I don't doubt that God honours the desire to work at unity and fellowship.

What happens next?

Friday 15th Feb
There was only Jude and I around for morning prayers today, the rest of the guys are down in Vranje. It's normally about 20 minutes to half an

hour. Today, we clocked up a good hour. I don't fully understand the reasons behind the sequence of the conversation, but we started on alternative medicine, raced on to divorce, diverted to yoga, headed through the murky waters of children conceived through rape, back on to acupuncture and ended up discussing the weather! Who'd have thought 1 Corinthians 8 could cover that much ground!

'What happens next?' is increasing in regularity in my (well, all of our) thought patterns at the mo. In two and a half months, I'll be unemployed and do not have faith that my six chord guitar repertoire will keep the bailiffs at bay for long! Have spoken to my Daddy, who spoke encouragingly about the 'numerous options open to me' – but frankly, it's rather tricky to notice any of them from here. What does a girl, who trained in sport psychology and has spent her last three years living and working in the relief world, do? I'm not a pro in anything. Familiar with pit latrines, septic tanks, gable ends in the Balkans, malnutrition rates in southern Sudan, have user competency with HF radios and sat-phones – but struggle with the tumble dryer; I can say sorry and thank you but little more in six languages – you see, skills and experiences that don't fit your bog standard job description too snugly! Yes, yes, all transferable. I do believe that God has plans for each of our lives, including mine, but I'm afraid I'll be chatting and miss it! Have come to the conclusion this week that I am not God's gift to field management. It's a wall, where's the door? ....time to 'faithfully wait on the Lord' – not a strength of mine.

I've never been too hot on keeping myself firmly rooted in the here and now. My last three years have run work-wise on a series of short-term contracts. My greatest spell of job security has been a lengthy stay of ten months in Kosovo – but even that was two five month contracts! There is an element of it being the nature of the work. No disaster or no role I can fill = no work. No funding, no project = no work. The consequence of that is that you arrive on a six month project, spend a couple of months settling in, a couple of months effectively getting on with your job and the last couple of months checking out the 'what next?' bit.

Trouble is, it gets a bit embarrassing when you're in the UK between projects and time after time people politely inquire, as they invariably do, 'What's next for you?' Depending on my mood, I have a raft of potential responses. There's the shallow one: 'For now it's lovely to have some time at home; I'm going to wait and see what comes up.' Then there's the slightly more cynical option: 'Just wait for the next disaster, I guess!'

The most genuine one, but unfortunately the one that the casual inquirer least wants to hear is: 'I'm not sure. It's doing my head in at the minute. I don't know if it's time to stop relief work and do something else; and if it is I haven't got a clue what that something is. There are so many elements of so many jobs I'd love to do, but they don't remotely fit in any neat packaging. I have loved relief work and have no idea what else I could possibly do that I would find so fulfilling, so part of me thinks I might as well carry on. The other part thinks it's not about me being fulfilled and I feel at times as though my compassion is wearing thinner than it was ...' Getting the gist of it?

Friday 22nd Feb

Training day: Leadership, team stuff and fraud. The fraud stuff was hard. So contra-trust. 'Any loopholes in your systems will be exploited.' What a thought... apparently there is no relationship between management confidence that fraud isn't occuring and actual fraud occurrence. That is frightening. I finished the session, better informed, but saddened by it all; such a 'dirty issue', hard stuff to hear. We have to trust our guys so much. The language issue alone makes us so potentially vulnerable. Most meetings are in Serbski, we don't actually have a clue what is said when we are translated – we trust them. Horrible to have to think of some of the possibilities.

Photo Exhibition

Held a photo exhibition of our beneficiaries today in Nis. Months of preparation.

19:52 – Enya is serenading, my glass of wine slipped unhindered down my throat. I'm loitering helpfully amidst display boards of photos and paintings, ready to offer assistance to anyone needing comment. No-one does. There is a steady trickle of guests showing a complete range of art appreciation from rapturous enthusiasm to yawning disinterest. During the official guest bit this afty we had beneficiaries, authorities, reps from other NGOs, our suppliers and contractors and our funders all under one roof looking at visual representations of the plight of refugees and IDPs in Serbia. Issues that have dropped out of the media lens in the last couple of years, but have not become any less real to these guys. The aim was to reraise awareness – job done. Well, in part. The photos are going to be used by Tearfund this summer at festivals and events round the country – I'm pooped.

Feel a little like I have when I've been involved in wedding days and then all of a sudden the bride and groom have gone. The guests are finding their coats and taking home the wrong cameras; and it's all done. Something of an exhausted anticlimax.

We cleared up completely in 17 minutes! Wow. The months of prep and hours of effort today has taken and we transformed our exhibition into an empty hall again in just 17 minutes! I got home to be greeted by the smell of mulled wine stewing on the stove – prepared by Mike; and my slippers placed by Gary, warming beside the stove. Lovely gestures from the guys of support and thoughtfulness. I was touched.

Got up to my room to find two balloons and a red thick pen message on a banner attached to my ceiling:
'WELL DONE EMMA'
Beautiful. A wonderful way to close the day.

In Serbia, the most striking impact of the exhibition certainly was with the families that we featured. Extra time was taken with each of them, to hear their stories, to report them accurately, to try to understand not only some of the issues that they faced during the conflict but those they continue to face today. It was incredible that all of our feature families managed to get in to Nis for the exhibition. Money obviously is not at a premium in these families and yet they all chose to go without something in order to make the trip into town. At the exhibition I chatted with one lady standing beside a display of photos of her family. She was wearing a dress, had put on make-up and done her hair. She looked starkly different from the lady the team had visited the week before with the invitations. I asked her why she had come: 'Because you (Tearfund) have tried to hear me and tell others about me and my family, to try to make a difference. None of the others (agencies) have done that.' Incredible.

Ski time

Thursday 28th Feb

21:08 I'm on my jollies! Have for the first time in a long time managed to maintain almost complete focus on work stuff until the end of the day pre-jollies! Mind you, was out the door by 16:50, well committed to the cause of rest and recuperation. Mike, Gary and I have had a lovely Chinese.

23:34 Packed. Peaceful. Pooped.

A friend emailed an analogy about the importance of taking breaks. It was about how we tend to keep on working away. Even when we start to become less efficient as we get more tired, all we do is increase our effort, get more tired and therefore less efficient and so on. It compared us to saws. As the saw becomes blunt, we don't notice and simply saw ever harder but ever less successfully. All we need to do is change the blade and start again – sharp. For me, changing our blades is so often about taking that break that in the short term you feel you can ill-afford but that in the long term you can't afford not to take.

I went skiing and came back with a very sharp, effective blade!

'I'm back!'

Had a thought provoking email from a friend today about choices. She
used to work for Tearfund but now works in the UK. It was about
how, when she was away, part of her longed for home; and now at
home, part of her longs for away. Hit a note with me. I have that
inevitable decision to take; it's on the horizon, yet steaming ever closer. The Serbian Inquisition from Dasic didn't help today. 'How will you
ever get married if you just keep moving on?' He has a point – but you
can't magic that, can you? You can engineer many events and opportunities in your life. But you can't map out the course and timing of
love, falling into it and having someone (ideally the same person)
'falling back' at the same time – I'm sounding like something from
Captain Corelli's Mandolin! Trouble is, the life I want seems to be
dichotomous; the security of 'home', the adventure of 'away'. That's
not a smooth continuum where you pick a comfy point of compro-
mise that gives you both, but one where you have to get one or
t'other. Not both. My big fear is making the wrong choice. Oh, for
writing on the wall! Thinking about emailing for more info about a
post advertised overseas, but have also thought about joining a volleyball club at home. Marvellous.

Out there

Towards the end of the project, I was able to spend ever increasing
amounts of time out of the office visiting families we were working
with. I loved it. It's one of the reasons that I got into this work in the
first place. But unfortunately, like so many other jobs such as teaching
or nursing, the longer you stay in it, the greater the potential to drift
away from your working 'coal face' and therefore ultimately to
move away from some of what initially drew you to that area of work.
My role had meant that I was at least one step removed from the actual people impacting nature of our work and I'd missed it. Getting out
with the project team was usually a highlight of my week.

Friday 22nd March
Met one of our older beneficiaries today. He lives by himself, (he drove trains for 41 years) and told us his story of the conflict, part of it anyway. He used to live near Pristina, the only Serb in an otherwise Kosovo-Albanian village. As the VJ (Serb army) and Serb Police approached the village in March/April '99, he represented the residents, pleading with the army and police not to harm them, not to burn homes, take prisoners, torture individuals or cause others to flee. They bypassed the village, leaving it and its residents unharmed. Months later, as the Serb forces left Kosovo and with them the vast majority of the former Kosovo-Serb population, his hero status left too. The whole village, bar one neighbour of his, all turned against him. Former friends and neighbours tortured him. The goodness and richness in their personal relationship was not strong enough to override the complete breakdown in the collective ethnic grouping relationship. He fled. He now lives alone in a one roomed house with little more than his memories. He cried as he spoke. The bit that gets me about it and pulls at something inside me, is that he and his neighbours lived at peace with one another for years, they were friends. Yet, as part of opposing political/ethnic groupings they couldn't do that, they became enemies. Same people but what they represented or were represented by were not compatible. No victors in war – none. Pedja was translating this story, tears in his eyes, chain-smoking vigorously. So much pain still, so much hurt and anguish. When it was time for us to say our goodbyes, we stood up. The usual handshake between Tearfund engineer and project beneficiary was replaced by a hug, a huge embrace – between two hurting men.

Wednesday 27th March
Wonderful moment in the Collective Centre – we have finally finished. It was the sign-off today – the 4th and finally successful attempt, quite a formal affair, clipboards all round. I was being a real girl and checking the fit of the toilet doors. We've put in a complete water and sanitation system and there I was checking to see if the loo doors closed properly! Anyway, as is predictable with this rather disappointing contractor the wood did not fit the hole. There I was outside the loo, doing my level

best to pull the door towards me. Gave it a good few slams with increasing volume and force, to no avail. Dasic had a go. He heaved the door towards him. Three ominous sequential noises followed.

- 'Chink-chink' – the key on the inside of the door wriggled free of the lock
- 'Clink-shhhh' – key hit tiles and slid
- 'Splash' – the one day old key plopped down the loo, following the newly installed S bend and squeaky clean pipes to the sewage connection.

Marvellous. Dasic looked at me, I at him, we both looked at the crowd of people that had gathered at the door. 'Sorry.' A lovely little ice breaker.

One of the residents came beaming up to me just before we left, wielding a bent coat hanger, sleeves rolled up, arms dripping wet and triumphantly waving the toilet key. As you can imagine, I was delighted to shake his hand as we said our goodbyes!

The Collective Centre being reconstructed

Had a cracking discussion about minority rights. An ethnic group moves into a country, settles, establishes themselves, grows in number, potentially becomes the numerical majority. What level of rights should they be entitled to – cultural freedom, language, education, etc? Tricky one, that. Interesting having Gary and Mike out here, hearing their opinions on South Africa and New Zealand. I've got to find my opinion on that.

Friday 29th March
'He hasn't done the roof. It says on his monitoring form......um, yup got it. Roof to be completed by 27th – it's the 29th. He's not done it.'

These were my words to Dasic as we drove down to Ramistar's place. Another disappointment. Another promise broken by a beneficiary. I mentally rolled my sleeves up, took a deep breath, set my face like flint and got out the car. I missed most of the words between the two men, but I understood the conversation – the gesticulations, expressions, tone, etc didn't leave much guess work needed to fill in the gaps. He felt unwell. His sons are doing paid work. He will do it – don't worry. He then grabbed my arm, hard and invited us in for coffee. I refused – he insisted. Dasic refused and tried to loosen Ramistar's grip on my arm – Ramistar insisted. We went in for a drink.

Ramistar and his family are displaced from Kosovo. They fled from their village nearly three years ago. He hasn't heard word from one of his sons who was captured there in 1998. Nothing for 4 years. Ramistar is one of the most beautiful, gentle men I have ever met. He must be mid-60's, maybe 70. He used to be a lawyer. He usually has an electric twinkle in his eyes and a face that explodes into joy when he smiles. Today no twinkle, no smile even – just pain, fear and exhaustion. The judge in Prokuplje told Ramistar recently that it was his own fault his son was missing. He should have protected his family better, had his son behind him, that way he couldn't have been taken. Ramistar punched him. He feels ashamed that he did.

He is hoping his son is still alive. He has had no body to bury, so in the meantime he has hope – not a lot, but enough not to give up. 15th April is the date when Kosovo-Serbs are to be released from Kosovo prisons; and Kosovo-Albanians from Serb prisons. All prisoners of war will be transferred to their homelands to continue their sentences. Ramistar is waiting for his son. Before that date a number of recovered Serbian bodies are being 'brought home'. They're also expecting a number of exhumed bodies to arrive in Serbia in the next few days. Dead or alive he's dying for news, he's living for news.

I asked Dasic how many Serbs were expected to be transferred on the 15th. He said a few thousand. I asked how many Albanian prisoners Serbia was holding, that would be released.
'About 350.'
'That's all?'
'Yes, that's all of them.'
I shuddered. The hairs on my neck stood up. The 1,500 missing men of Gjakove – and yet only 350 allegedly in Serb prisons. And that's from all of Kosovo. The sums don't add up. How many men like Ramistar on both sides of the border are still waiting?

He hasn't done the roof. It didn't matter so much. All things are relative.

By this stage, the project team had been working with some of the beneficiaries for as long as six months. Some of their relationships were incredibly strong. Our engineers were more than just technicians. Our logisticians were more than delivery men. Our social workers were more than infrequent visitors. Towards the end of the project, many of our beneficiaries would speak about the way their lives had been 'kick started'; how the project had given them hope. Projects don't do that by themselves. People need to be involved for that to happen. I am hugely proud of the way the team gave of themselves in that way. It's the result of investment, of bothering again and again, to connect, to hear the stories, to understand.

There is a chocolate factory near Prokuplje, geographically central to where the project was working. Members of the team would buy small bags of chocolate, or coffee, or cigarettes that they would share with the families. That extra mile isn't on job descriptions. The joy and satisfaction of seeing a house completed, after months of work and support and co-operation, was often tempered by the inevitable sadness that there was no longer any reason to visit. It didn't stop these families ringing the office for a chat!

Easter

Sunday 31st March

Kinder Easter eggs for brekky in the absence of any real eggs. My Mummy had made me a card, which is now on the hotel window sill, a perfectly relevant visual aid for the talky bit for our Easter Service. The three crosses on the hill. That's what I'm going to talk about, not the mocker, or Jesus (well a bit about Jesus) – but mainly the criminal that recognises Jesus for who he is.

We're in Sarajevo for the Easter team break. It is an incredible city – for centuries it was a celebration of ethnic compatibility and harmony as mixed people groups lived side by side. Until '92 that was – a decade ago. I was doing my A levels when Bosnia 'kicked off'. I do remember feeling incredibly frustrated and ignorant at my lack of understanding as to who was who and who was fighting who and why? Ten years on, I'm a little clearer.

In a sector of the old town there is a mosque, a Catholic church, a synagogue and an Orthodox church, literally within spitting distance of each other, maybe 200m apart. Today people can worship at each of these. 10 years ago, almost to the day, the siege started. A horrific bloody time of Balkan history that has fascinated me this weekend as we have trawled through the background section of the Lonely Planet guide. We took coffee outside a cafe by the river and there was not a cloud in the blue sky as the sun lowered itself gently. We sat looking at the bridge that an aristocratic Austrian was shot on, triggering the start of the 1st world war.

It makes you wonder, if he'd stayed on one side of the river, where 20th century history would have gone! The city is still peppered with the scars of a more recent war – a silent reminder amidst the vibrancy of a place and a people getting on with the business of living.

Flip, we are tired. People are dropping off snoozing every time they sit down long enough. Beyond 9pm we're losing all social skills. Noticed how often we are nipping at each other. Good to have time away from work.

Wednesday 3rd April
We've finished a mammoth two hour team Bibley, worshippy, prayery time. Struck by something a very good friend mentioned in an email that came through this morning. She said 'God has faith in us' – that's all. God has faith in us. I'd never twigged that before. Here I am praying for my faith to grow. I'd never seen it the other way around that God has faith, in us – in me! There's a passage in the book of Hebrews that talks about

- By faith how Noah built an ark when it wasn't even raining!
- By faith Abraham went where he was called even though he did not know where he was going.
- By faith Moses' parents hid him in spite of the King's edict.

Thinking about the converse side of the story:

- By faith God built his church on Peter – the hot-headed, impulsive chap who denied Jesus three times.
- By faith God assembled a rabble of 12 assorted blokes to 'go and make disciples of all nations'.
- By faith God used Paul a previous persecutor of Christians to develop his church.

Amazing. He believed in these guys. With his power and love and grace working in and through me, he believes in me. Not my power – his. He loves me and has faith in me. There you have it......

Saturday 6th April

Full on work day. I finally left the office at 4ish, absolutely shattered. Gary gave me a lift home, I poured myself two mugs of tea and collapsed in the chair – mug in each hand. Thought about having a bath, or reading, doing my log, sorting about my washing but opted to sit. Not do anything. As I switched off, I began to pray, a rambling, stop starty, unfocussed prayer, full of distractions and daydreams. I realised that every time I have spare time I fill it, relaxing but always doing something. I never stop completely and 'tarry awhile' – great phrase. Then I get ridiculously frustrated I never hear God. Not surprising, he probably can't get through – the line's busy! So I 'tarried', for an hour or so. Supped my tea from each mug alternately, sat quietly, prayed a bit, threw a log on the fire and tarried some more. Picked up my Bible at one stage and opened it at 1 Peter. Read a bit and this verse leapt out at me:

'Each one should use whatever gift he has received to serve others, faithfully administering God's grace in its various forms' (1 Pet. 4:10)

Funny, with all of this what's next? stuff going down for all of us, I realised that I have become focussed on the wrong things, focussed on the organisation, the role and the status, rather than simply doing what I can do to serve others with what God has given me. That's what you get when you just sit! Must do it more often.

Evaluation Team

Tuesday 9th April

Cracking day. The evaluation team and I had a meeting with our donor – he loves us! Yes, the man I insulted to his face recently for being a 'nagging male Serb' was singing our praises. Visited some of our beneficiaries, I was floored by what one of the guys had done. I'd seen the house a few months ago. He was intending to move his family upstairs into what was then an unsealed, draughty, concrete floored, semi-open attic. Now it is phenomenal. He has used the materials we gave them, as a kick start and has matched our investment and then some with his own and borrowed money from his family. It looks superb, I could not believe that the empty, cold, building site could look so much like a home in so short a time. His children love the space they have to play in. I asked him what had changed since he had been able to have some space for his family. 'I can walk around in my pants now!' I'd said weeks ago I'd have a raki with him when he'd finished. I did.

Friday 12th April
I managed to get through to my Mummy and Daddy on the phone this morning – it's their anniversary. I've been trying to work out what I should say to two people who have managed lovingly to live together for that many years and produce two children who delight in going 'home – to the rock' as much as Sara and I do. I think it's a combination of 'congratulations, great effort, keep up the good work and thank you.' It's funny, so often you hear of parents being proud of their children, their successes, their achievements and who they have become. Don't often hear the converse said, how proud children are of their parents. I am.

I feel a real sense of family within the expat team at the moment. I think all of us are working hard at the here and now of work stuff, yet have half an eye on the fact that within three weeks, Team Serbia will be history. 8-18 months people have been together out here, SO hard to walk away from that. Enjoying it while it lasts. I'm aware of the tendency we humans, myself included, have to back off from those we love pre-separation, determined not to miss out on the now, though trying to protect myself from 'then'.

Saturday 13th April
Final chat with the evaluators. Out for dinner and feedback from the guys. Mike inadvertently tumbled a glass of red wine over the table and my sleeve. He reacted swiftly to the comments of 'tip salt on it' and grabbed a cruet in a flash and started heavily dusting both my arm and the table cloth. 'Mike, that's pepper!' I was interested in the evaluators' comments but unfortunately found that at 10:00pm on Saturday night, my concentration on all things strategy, technical and political was frankly abysmal. My distractedness was heightened further when Mike and I

became aware that we could pierce the little round cakes of bread with the kebab skewer like two wheel axles with the intention of putting a plate on them – like a car. Our efforts were thwarted by Captain Sensible (Gary) – which, as he took our bread cakes away from us, only induced a further bout of the giggles.

Evaluations are an odd experience – on one hand you're trying to present a completely open view of the project, so the evaluators 'see it as it is' and we can all make the most of this 'mutual learning opportunity'. On the other hand, you want to minimise the bad and accentuate the good. Eventually, largely due to the fact I was getting on so well with Jane and Malcolm (the evaluators), they got the lot – as it was. The project had generally gone well, so the opportunity to view it with the help of fresh pairs of eyes was great. Of course, there are things that could be done better next time, but that's fine too. The guys were both sensitive enough to put those things across in non-abrasive ways. By the end of their trip, I was sorry to see them go.

Monday April 15th
360 bodies worth of human remains (Kosovo-Serbs) have been exhumed and taken to the Serbia-Kosovo border today for identification. That's a mass of human remains that have been buried for three years; dug up, transported and placed for relatives and friends to try and recognise. I have no idea quite how quickly the body decomposes. I don't think there'd still be any soft tissue, skin or hair; more likely just skeletal bone, maybe jewellery, clothes and shoes. Thousands of families with missing relatives, including Ramistar and his family, are there hoping for some conclusive proof that their suspended reality of waiting is over. Appalling.

Tuesday April 16th
Was out today, monitoring with Sladja. Was awed at one point. We employed the engineers to do technical surveys, monitor, provide tech support etc. Watched Sladja and wanted to be a fly on the wall and not interrupt what was going on. It was brilliant. The 1st house we were at, the door opened and a two-year old boy ran up to her legs, flung

himself at them, calling 'Sladja, Sladja!' Whilst she sat and chatted with the adults, he climbed all over her, playing with her fingernails, 'drawing' on the file etc. His granny had made two lace baskets for Sladja and I and hardened them in a sugar solution. She'd spent days on them – because she wanted to say thank you.

The next house, the old man was in by himself and as we said goodbye and walked to the gate, they shook hands and shared a joke. Then he picked his tulips growing in the garden for us – to say thank you.

The third place, a girl of 7ish ran up to us as we walked to their house 'Sladja……. kupatilo….. super!' 'The bathroom is super', Sladja translated; she'd had many baths already. We did our sign-off and stayed for about twenty minutes. The girl was having problems with her maths homework and her Mum didn't know how to help. Sladja took her through it step by step. The Mum and Sladja hugged as they said goodbye. It's fantastic to see the depth of relationship that our team have with the beneficiaries. All of this is above and beyond their job spec – but it's this that makes this project so special; the fact that our staff will now stay in touch with many of the families they have worked with. I was moved to silence watching all this go on – all in a day's work for Sladja, an Aunty; a friend, a teacher – not just an engineer.

Wednesday April 17th
Signed off one family today, Deljanin Vukomir. He was tearful with thanks. I asked him how his family were doing. There are 8 of them – Granny and Grandad, Deljanin and his wife and 4 young sons. None of them are employed. No income. Only three of the boys are eligible for food assistance from the authorities. The monthly allowance per person is:

    Two litres oil
    2kg sugar
    12kg flour

Sounds reasonable per person, but stretch three lots of that between 8… it doesn't go far. I was chatting with Deljanin as his wife ducked back into the house. I could see her through the open door looking round her room. Her eyes settled on two glass ornaments – she picked them up, brought them outside and gently placed them in my hands. This family, living below the breadline, with little hope at the moment of making ends meet, gave me two of their ornaments.

Out of the 360 bodies, 5 have been positively identified through forensic testing. 5. I'm floored by this. Remember watching footage of the foot and mouth cattle pyres last year; and feeling repulsed. That was cattle. Ramistar has found nothing, no-one. His son is still missing.

There's still little I can say about this. The figures speak clearly for themselves. Only five bodies positively identified, 355 not. I do not understand at what stage you can let go of someone, having no proof that they are dead. What are your options? Ever dwindling, yet never quite diminishing hope? Letting go and grieving for someone inconclusively that maybe, perhaps, possibly, you do not need to grieve for?

It grieves my heart that these losses – missing sons, brothers, fathers in the Balkans – weren't accidents or acts of nature. They were simply at the hands of man. At some point, someone decided to capture, perhaps torture and possibly kill those missing men. Man has chosen to hurt man in ways that, for those left behind, will probably leave a pain that time will not erase.

Wednesday 24th April
Gave a speech today to some refugees we've been working with. I spoke about how I've chosen to leave England for now and yet my heart is still very much there; so how much more their hearts must remain in the places they have had no choice other than to leave. Then I spoke briefly about the choice they now have of looking backwards with anger, sorrow, grief and loss or of acknowledging those things, yet resolving to look forward and invest as much of their heart as they can into here and now. There were a number of hearty grunts, understanding nods, smiles and even some tears back. Hard to connect with people who are hurting and grieving so much still.

Nearing the end

Monday 29th April

As a team, the 4 of us are 'taking' the local church service on Wednesday.
We've split up who's doing what. Gary on intro, me preaching, Mike giving a testimony and Jude on prayers. There you have it. I've never
preached.

Tuesday 30th April

Have just spent about three fruitless hours trying to prepare a preach on
the wise and foolish builders. In spite of all human effort I could muster
– I'm absolutely clueless and uninspired. No problem, there'll still be 12
hours when I wake up – most of them filled with other things, but still
12 hours!

Wednesday 1st May

Lay in bed this morning looking intently at my ceiling 'Oh God.... I
do not have a clue how to do this preach.' Lay there and literally
within a few minutes, ideas were coming in thick and fast. Couldn't
believe it! I tried SO hard last night; then as soon as I stop trying....
progress!

I've had some fantastically encouraging emails this week. There are the
usual faithful hard core who I know will be in touch. But this week,
those good friends whose correspondence could fairly be described as
sporadic got in touch, to wish me well as we close down. Makes a big
difference.

I did Goca's debrief today. The team have been incredibly open with me
about how they're feeling, their thoughts on the management of the programme, Tearfund leaving and their futures. It's not one of those urgent
things on the list, but I'm determined to have one on one time with each
of them before we go. It has been a real pleasure to work with them.
Going to be hard to say goodbye.

We walked into church 10 minutes before the start of the service. I was expecting 50-100 people. It was packed. 350-400 was the estimate. Right. No problem. Not enough seats, people were standing! We were ushered down to the front and sat down. There was a verse up on the OHP, I think it was to try and keep a bit of quiet:

1 Corinthians 14:33 – 'For God is not a God of disorder but of peace' My eyes went down the text to the next verse in my Bible – 'Women should remain silent in the churches. They are not allowed to speak…..'

Not the greatest of encouragements minutes before speaking!

Gary introduced us, Tearfund and the project in his usual engaging way, then called me up. After the stresses and strains of getting the stuff together, actually delivering it was great fun. I enjoyed it. Mickey gave an incredibly honest testimony. Jude wrapped it all up in prayer – fantastic!

I had a powerful but gentle sense of conviction that my lack of involvement in the local church over the last 8 months is, frankly, appalling. I know I didn't feel welcomed when I first went, language was a barrier, the lack of joy in the church was a massive turn off, etc. but to have gone to church three times in 8 months over here – not good! I became acutely aware of the fellowship I could have been part of and had chosen not to be.

Conviction is a powerful thing. I used to think of it in terms of that slightly – yet not very – guilty twinge you get the morning after you have stealthily crept around different gardens on the way home from the pub uprooting 'For Sale' signs and transferring them to the gardens of other properties that were not for sale.

The conviction I felt that day in church was different. So quiet. Such gentleness, no fudging of the issue, no diluting it, or watering it down – but absolute clarity. It reminded me of the passage in John 8 (3-11) where Jesus is presented with a woman caught in adultery. He doesn't condemn her. Nor does he condone her actions. He manages to protect her from the judgement and punishment of the crowd around her, yet also expose her sin and then offers her some hope for the future, a way out – 'Go now and leave your life of sin' (Jn. 8:11).

Thursday 2nd May

We've all had some positive feedback today about last night's service. I loved it, I loved the whole thing, praying about it, prepping it, delivering it – the works, made me tick like you would not believe. I know I have to be incredibly careful not to allow my ego – that at times inflates more readily than a beach ball – to get carried away. I was feeling guilty that I'd liked it so much! I sat quietly praying today and felt God gently say to me 'Emma, it's OK to enjoy it. That's what I want!' Sometimes it is so easy to get our Christianity skewed and believe that God will only put us through trying and testing situations, where there will be an element of uncomfortableness, so that we will grow in him. I know with something like last night the honour and glory all goes to God, but that doesn't mean I can't enjoy it with a passion, relish the opportunity and get massively excited! Fantastic. What a chance eh? To speak to people about Jesus, his Lordship and our responsibility to respond to that. And to love doing it – bonus!

It's like I've got a new pair of eyes on this week. Our wagons roll out of Nis on Tuesday (if all is well), so effectively this is our last week here. I'm looking at the scenery and being wowed by it – this place is phenomenal on the eye, the rivers, the mountains, the plains, the hills – awe-inspiring. And the people, their warmth, their humour, their love. I feel like a sponge at the moment, wanting to squeeze up every last drop of here, make the most of everything, every opportunity. To spend time with people, to watch the sunset on the balcony, to play tennis, to get up and see the sun rise – I want it all, I want to pack these last few days with as much of 'Serbia' as I can. I do not want to leave. I want to arrive home, but I do not want to leave.

Close down

Friday 3rd May

That's it then. Tearfund Nis office is closed. I sat on the steps holding the polystyrene pin charts that have directed the efforts of my waking working hours over the last few months. How many jobs are there that you close down completely rather than you leave the job? Not a lot. I'm a bit pooped. The local guys were flagging today. It was a scorcher and they asked to go for a picnic at lunchtime (i.e. for the afternoon). I said no. It didn't go down well. There's no way we'd have got it all done otherwise. As it is, there's still plenty to keep me off the streets over the weekend!

They've left the office for the last time; it's quiet in here now. We've finished.

Saturday 4th May

I decided at 12:10 in impulsive Em style that I wanted to buy 'a little something' for each of the team, to give out at the leaving dinner tonight. Not the smartest timing in the world, we were due at Maja's at 12:30, it's Orthodox Easter weekend so the shops closed at two or in some cases three o'clock. Had no idea what to get people, so it was all a bit of a rush. That said I managed to get 9 gifts bought within 56 minutes!

I was taking photos all evening, but even they will not do justice to the atmosphere. I couldn't have planned a better final team 'do'. We were in short sleeves all night, a musical quartet were superbly performing to our table, the food was delicious, the setting typically Balkan. Between the salads and the meat course we were up dancing, Dasic, Slobo and Pedja lent their voices to the quartet, others were chatting away, such a relaxed atmosphere. I have never had a night like it, so very Balkan, so very Serbia.

Gary, Mike, Jude and I gave thank you and goodbye speeches, certificates, T-shirts and a programme photo CD. The guys gave each of us a lovely pen and an address book with each of their contact details in and strict instructions to use it! Inevitably the evening came to an end. Goodbyes. For so many weeks we've been going flat out to reach the finish, but the sweet joy of completing is accompanied by the bitter grief of leaving.

Prolonged combinations of the Balkan three kisses and the English hugs, sometimes with many words, sometimes with few.

Sunday 5th May

Went to church this morning which was good. I sat on the stage stairs at the end of the service and felt a big well of sadness rising. I think it was delayed tears from last night too. It's a protracted week of goodbyes, one after another. Usually, I feel like this a few weeks after I get home. I don't want to be upset and bring everyone else down with me, but I want to be real. I remember starting my Serbia log in tears of goodbye – here they are again.

The twin pangs of joy and sorrow. Sorrow to be leaving, to have finished, to go. Joy to be arriving home, to have completed what we came to do, at what might be next. Driving out of Serbia at the start of our journey taking the vehicles back to the UK across Europe, I seemed to be feeling them both, strongly, almost at the same time. The sense of relief that the stress was all over was powerful. I had next to no responsibility now. The realisation was sinking in that I was now leaving behind the people and place that had become so familiar to me. There was excitement that within a week or so I'd be at home, catching up again with friends and family. There was also concern that in a few weeks I'd be unemployed – what next? And there was the joy that the four of us had a week ahead with next to no pressure – a grand team finale, ominously lapping waves of tiredness and elation that the project had worked.

The trip home was awesome. Serbia, Croatia, Slovenia, Austria, Germany, France, onto the ferry – then over to the left hand side of the road. The best part of it was having the opportunity to spend time with Mike, Jude and Gary purely as friends.

The 'Afterword' Afterwards

I've been back in the UK now for three and a half months. It's always an interesting time of readjustment, post-assignment. No different this time. Friends have been remarkably tolerant of my various Titanic swings of thought across a spectrum of areas. This week, I assured my long suffering housemate that I wasn't going skiing in March, two days later I paid my deposit. I told her how I'd flatly refused to consider a potential job opportunity, only to express my 'keen interest and availability' the next day. I chatted to her about not wanting to go overseas for a while, then reeled off an enthusiastic harebrained plan to spend a few months re-travelling the apostle Paul's journeys (well, some of them) and write a book about it.

Other than these hopefully short-lived erratic irregularities to my psyche, these assignments have left other marks, other scars. I have touched death and observed war at close quarters. I've witnessed the venom of hatred and had to acknowledge desperate, seemingly hopeless situations. I've recognised how in many ways we can do so little to make significant changes; and seen the struggles of the church to be real and relevant through difficult times. I've lived amongst the effect of greed, the quest for power and control; lived in fear; and come face to face with some of the less desirable traits of who I am that have spilled under pressure.

The apostle Paul in his letter to the church in Galatia wrote of the acts of the sinful nature. Even though I was not necessarily prepared for these, it was my expectation that this is what conflict and disaster zones would show me; the worst of this world, the most desperate, messed up, evil aspects of human life. I was right – I saw these things. I lived amongst these things, I committed some of these acts and have been indelibly touched by them.

Sexual immorality – hearing of the pain of victims of rape during conflict – 'collateral damage'.

Impurity and debauchery – the extent of torture man will indulge in.

Idolatry and witchcraft – still practised in Sudan.

Hatred – the willingness with which man will destroy man.

Discord – the breakdown of relationships and trust within the team in Kosovo.

Jealousy – the desire for 'more', resulting in forcibly taking from others.

Fits of rage – the guys who lashed out crippling beatings with sticks.

Selfish ambition – my desire to succeed for my sake rather than for the people we were serving.

Dissensions – the petty grumblings I was part of within teams.

Factions and envy – The lack of trust the Army had for various allied groups.

Drunkenness – the frightening unpredictability of the Sudanese Military Commander.

But I guess wherever you are in the world, examples of this sort are not rare.

What I was not expecting was the flip side of the coin. Further down the chapter in Galatians, Paul contrasts this sinful nature with the God-given fruit of the Spirit; the good bits, the right, the true, the hopeful, the just. It's the incredible presence of these in the places I have been, or more accurately the presence of these in the people I have been amongst, that has moved me more.

Love – amongst my teammates who committed to love each other in spite of ourselves.

Joy – in the faces of the grinning malnourished children playing in the dirt with buckets and spades in the feeding centre.

Peace – within the Pastor preaching the gospel whilst his nation raged at war.

Patience – in my colleagues who believed in, were working towards and awaiting a future less bloody than their past.

Kindness – from the family who shared the few nuts, roots and fruit they had with the visiting *Aluel*.

Goodness – finding a desire to forgive; or for some, desiring the desire to forgive.

Faithfulness – from the driver who prioritised the safety of the Tearfund team above his family during a time of insecurity.

Gentleness – in the hand of the elderly lady who comforted me, without any words.

Self-control – from the Kosovo-Albanian man explaining the road block to me whilst he still grieved for his family.

Whilst I was choosing the title for this book, I wanted to get across the nature of a double, indeed multi-edged sword of these various experiences. *Famines and Face Packs* – as I hope the rest of the book does – conveys something of the 'extra' and the 'ordinary'; the poverty and the richness; the humour and the very real tragedy; the despair that in so many cases was eased and extinguished by the hope and faith of belief in God and the application of that belief. Hoping for a lot, then, Ems – nothing new!

Photo: David Sterry

If you wish to explore the possibility of arranging a speaking engagement with Emma, email strattonem@yahoo.com